travelling
food

❖

Kay Francis

travelling

menus for leisure food

photography by Gerry Colley

NH
NEW
HOLLAND

First published in Australia in 2002 by
New Holland Publishers (Australia) Pty Ltd
Sydney • Auckland • London • Cape Town

14 Aquatic Drive Frenchs Forest NSW 2086 Australia
218 Lake Road Northcote Auckland New Zealand
86 Edgware Road London W2 2EA United Kingdom
80 McKenzie Street Cape Town 8001 South Africa

10 9 8 7 6 5 4 3 2 1

National Library of Australia Cataloguing-in-Publication Data:

Francis, Kay, 1952-.
   Travelling food.

   Includes index.
   ISBN 1 86436 757 1.

   1. Quick and easy cookery. 2. Outdoor cookery. I. Title.

   641.575

Publishing Manager: Anouska Good
Senior Editor: Monica Ban
Designer: Caroline Verity
Production Controller: Wendy Hunt
Reproduction: Colourscan, Singapore
Printer: Kyodo Printing, Singapore

Photograph credits: Green kettle on page 109, hat and chair on page 110
and Dutch oven on page 116 by Kay Francis.

For Anna and Jamie, who are always inspiring
...and for Philip, who like me, loves the outdoors

preface

'...many's the long night I've dreamed of
cheese—toasted, mostly...'

BEN GUNN IN *TREASURE ISLAND* ROBERT LOUIS STEVENSON (1850-1894)

The marooned Ben Gunn had been eating goats and berries and oysters for three years and longed for the simple comfort of melted cheese.

I remember craving fragrant hot scones with raspberry jam and lashings of whipped cream during a time spent camping on the beach of a Greek island. Nearby were fields of sun-ripened tomatoes and watermelon, and waterfront tavernas from whose kitchens drifted spicy aromas, but my appetite sought the unobtainable.

Fresh air and exercise, a change of environment, the liberation of mind space from routine, and time for leisure are all circumstances that trigger the appetite. A long drive is punctuated by refreshment stops, a camping trip revolves around meal times, planning to spend even just two winter days at a holiday cottage gives licence to thoughts of comforting indulgence. Boating, riding and walking are all activities made even more appealing by the anticipation of something delicious at the end. Picnicking is the most decadent food-driven outdoor activity—there is absolutely no need to pretend to be the slightest bit energetic—why else do we take rugs and cushions and wine?

Even for the most spontaneous excursion, a little planning and sharing of the food enhances the event for all. The menu ideas in *Travelling Food* are intended as triggers—follow them, or merely use them to devise your own schemes. If time for cooking is limited, supplement your efforts with purchased treats. The idea is to get out and enjoy the world, and at the same time eat whatever you desire—you are limited only by your imagination.

spring

summer 48

boating

riding

autumn 86

winter 124

holiday house cooking

winter walks

picnic baskets

at seven for six (breakfast)

after the rain (morning tea)

in the fields (lunch)

kite flying (afternoon tea)

symphony under the stars (dinner)

~

spring barbecues

under the trees (brunch)

in the courtyard (lunch)

with cocktails (late lunch)

early evening (dinner)

spring

at seven for six

(BREAKFAST)

'The year's at the spring,
And day's at the morn;
Morning's at seven;
The hillside's dew-pearled;
The lark's on the wing;
The snail's on the thorn:
God's in His Heaven–
All's right with the world!'

'THE YEAR'S AT SPRING' FROM *PIPPA PASSES*

ROBERT BROWNING (1812-1889)

Iced Strawberry Lassi with Rosewater

1½ cups (375ml/12fl oz) cultured buttermilk
250g (8oz) strawberries, hulled
1½ cups (375ml/12fl oz) natural
    full-cream yoghurt
1 tablespoon rosewater
6 large ice cubes
18 mint leaves, crushed, plus sprigs for garnish

Combine buttermilk, strawberries, yoghurt, rosewater and ice cubes in a blender and process until thick and smooth. Pour into a container with screw top leaving about 2cm (¾in) empty. Freeze mixture overnight. Remove from freezer first thing next morning, to allow mixture to become slushy and pourable. Pack centrally in picnic basket as a chiller block for other contents.

To serve, place crushed mint leaves into glasśes and pour lassi over. Garnish with mint sprigs.
MAKES 4 CUPS

mixture to make six omelettes, stacking them when turning out.

Combine filling ingredients, divide into six portions and place one portion in centre of top omelette (have browned side out). Fold in edges to form a parcel. Tie with 1 or 2 chives to secure. Wrap in waxed paper and stack in a lidded carrying container. Chill until required. Pack lemon wedges in a snap-lock plastic bag.
MAKES 6

note: To make Lemon Cream, combine ½ cup (125ml/4fl oz) crème fraîche or sour cream with the grated rind and juice of 1 lemon.

Omelette Parcels of Salmon Roe and Crab Meat in Lemon Cream

12 free-range eggs
½ cup dill tips
Finely grated rind of 1 medium lemon
30g (1oz) butter

Filling
500g (1 lb) crab meat (blue swimmer),
    picked over to remove shell fragments
3 tablespoons salmon roe
3 tablespoons Lemon Cream (see note)
6-12 long chives
Lemon wedges for garnish

Whisk eggs until fluffy. Stir in dill and lemon rind. Heat a large frying pan (non-stick if possible) over moderate heat. Rub surface of pan with butter (hold butter in a scrunched up piece of baking paper or use a pastry brush). Pour in egg to thinly coat pan (tip pan as you pour egg in, to distribute it evenly). Cook until set, then turn out onto a board (turn pan and let omelette fall, don't try and lift it). Repeat with remaining

Asparagus and Prosciutto Rolls

18 spears asparagus
125g (4oz) butter, at room temperature
¼ cup chopped tarragon
12 slices white bread
12 slices prosciutto

Preheat oven to 180°C (350°F/Gas Mark 4).
Blanch the asparagus, then halve the spears. Combine butter and tarragon and spread on one side of each slice of bread. Remove crusts.
Wrap three pieces of asparagus in a slice of prosciutto, then roll in a slice of bread, with buttered side exposed. Place, edges down, in one layer in a buttered baking dish and bake for 15-20 minutes until crisp and golden. Transport in dish or transfer to another container.
SERVES 6

note: Process crusts in a blender or food processor to make breadcrumbs. Freeze until required.

Little Fennel and Haloumi Tarts with Lemon Cream

Pastry

1¼ cups (190g/6oz) plain flour

1 teaspoon dried yeast

¼ teaspoon salt

¼ teaspoon ground cumin

½ cup (125ml/4fl oz) warm milk

2 tablespoons olive oil

1 egg, beaten, for glaze

Filling

½ cup fennel bulb, finely diced

60g (2oz) haloumi, finely diced

1 teaspoon preserved lemon, finely diced

1 tablespoon sour cream

For pastry, combine flour, yeast, salt and cumin in a bowl. Make a well in centre and pour in milk and oil. Stir to combine, then knead about 10 minutes. Shape into a ball, place in a lightly oiled ceramic or glass bowl, turn dough to oil surface. Cover with a clean tea towel (kitchen cloth) and stand in a warm, draft-free position for one hour, or until dough is doubled in bulk.

Preheat oven to 180°C (350°F/Gas Mark 4).

Punch down dough, turn onto a floured surface and knead briefly, then roll as thinly as possible (the dough should be less than 3mm (⅛in) thickness.

Cut into 24 x 6cm (2½in) squares. Brush pastry with beaten egg, then place a spoonful of the combined filling ingredients in centre of 12 squares. Top these with remaining pastry squares and press edges together to seal. Prick tops with a fork, brush with remaining egg, then lift tarts onto a baking tray.

Bake for 20 minutes until golden, cool on a wire rack, then pack into a lidded carrying container. Serve with Lemon Cream (see note opposite) passed separately.

SERVES 6

note: Lemon Cream is also good with Lemon and Cardamom Syrup Cakes (p26).

after the rain

'I, the puddle king of Avalon...'

JIM COLLEY, AGE 3 YEARS

Maple Pecan Cakes

200g (6½oz) pecan halves
125g (4oz) butter, at room temperature
1 cup (220g/7oz) raw caster sugar
3 free-range eggs, at room temperature
¼ cup (60ml/2fl oz) pure maple syrup
1½ cups (225g/7½oz) self-raising flour, sifted
½ cup (125ml/4fl oz) cultured buttermilk

Preheat oven to 180°C (350°F/Gas Mark 4).
   Roast pecans until just crisp, about 10 minutes.
Reserve 12, then crush remainder (cool, then
place in a large snap-lock plastic bag and crush
with rolling pin).
   Combine remaining ingredients in large bowl of
an electric mixer and beat to mix thoroughly.
Increase speed and beat 2–3 minutes until smooth
and pale. Stir in nuts.
   Butter 18 x ⅓ cup (90ml/3fl oz) moulds or
muffin tins. Place a pecan half in the base of
each, then spoon cake mixture over top, to
three-quarters full.
   Bake 20 minutes, until golden. Cool in tins for
5 minutes, then turn out onto a wire rack to cool
completely. Store in an airtight container.
MAKES 18

note: Depending on the shape of your tins,
you may wish to decorate the top of each cake
with a pecan half.

Chocolate Chip Tarts

150g (5oz) butter, at room temperature
1 cup (150g/5oz) plain flour
½ cup (60g/2oz) icing sugar
¼ cup (60g/2oz) dark chocolate chips
⅓ cup (65g/2½oz) brown sugar
½ teaspoon vanilla essence

Beat 125g (4oz) butter with flour and icing sugar,
to form a smooth dough. Pinch off walnut-sized
pieces, roll into balls and press into small non-
stick muffin tins, taking care to keep bases intact.
Chill for 15 minutes.
   Preheat oven to 150°C (300°F/Gas Mark 2).
   Distribute chocolate chips evenly between
pastry cases. Melt remaining butter, whisk with
brown sugar and vanilla until thick. Spoon
carefully into cases, over chocolate chips.
   Bake for 20 minutes, or until pastry is pale
golden. Cool in tins. Gently twist tarts to
loosen them, then remove carefully. Store in
an airtight container.
MAKES 18

Apricot Heart Shortbiscuits

125g (4oz) butter
⅓ cup (75g/2½oz) caster sugar
3 egg yolks
½ teaspoon apricot or vanilla essence
1½ cups (225g/7oz) plain flour
250g (8oz) apricot fruit leather (or apricot jam)

Preheat oven to 160°C (325°F/Gas Mark 3).
 Cream butter and sugar until light and fluffy.
Beat in yolks and essence. Stir in sifted flour and
a pinch of salt to form a soft dough. Shape into
a disc, wrap in plastic and chill for 20 minutes.
Roll between two large sheets of baking paper to
3mm (⅛in) thickness. Cut into 6cm (2½in) hearts.
Using a 4cm (1½in) heart cutter, cut out centre of
half the hearts to make frames. Re-roll cut-out
dough to make more biscuits. Cut 4cm (1½in)
hearts from fruit leather. Place a fruit leather
heart on centre of whole heart, then position the
cut heart 'frame' on top.
 Lift onto buttered or non-stick oven trays and
bake for 15 minutes, or until pale golden. Lift onto
wire racks to cool. Store in an airtight container.
MAKES 24

in the fields

'It was Spring, the fickle Spring; an' a most amazin' thing
Came upon me sudden-like an' set me marvellin'.'

'A FREAK OF SPRING' FROM *JIM OF THE HILLS* C.J. DENNIS (1876-1938)

Crumbed Pork Strips

2 cups (100g/3½oz) fresh breadcrumbs
½ cup fresh tarragon leaves
½ cup (75g/2½oz) finely grated Parmesan
4 cloves garlic
12-16 (560-750g/18½oz) pork medallions
½ cup (75g/2½oz) plain flour, seasoned
    with salt and freshly ground black pepper
3 large free-range eggs, beaten
125g (4oz) butter
½ cup (125ml/4fl oz) olive oil
2 tablespoons diced preserved lemon,
    for garnish

Process crumbs with tarragon, Parmesan and
garlic in a blender or food processor. Press both
sides of each medallion into seasoned flour, then
dip into egg to coat, then press into breadcrumbs.
Place on baking tray and refrigerate at least
10 minutes (meat can be prepared 24 hours in
advance and refrigerated in a covered container).

  To cook, heat a heavy-based frying pan over a
moderate heat. Add half each of the butter and
oil. Fry pork in batches, on both sides, until
golden. Replenish butter and oil when required.
Cool pork on paper towels, then cut into 2cm
(¾in) wide strips. Pack into a lidded carrying
container, for transportation. Pass preserved
lemon separately.
SERVES 6

Beetroot Leaf with Garlic

Leafy tops and stalks from 4 beetroot
    (use from next recipe)
4-6 cloves garlic, crushed
½ cup (125ml/4fl oz) verjuice
¼ cup (60ml/2fl oz) extra virgin olive oil

Wash, drain, and then roughly slice beetroot tops
and stalks into 2cm (¾in) wide ribbons and
pieces. Place in a deep, heavy-based frying pan
with remaining ingredients. Cover and simmer
over a low heat for 30 minutes. Cool, then
transfer to a lidded carrying container. Serve at
room temperature with soft white cheese, such as
feta or chèvre, and crusty bread.
SERVES 6-8

Pickled Beetroot

4 medium beetroot, trimmed to leave about
    2cm (³⁄₄in) stalk attached (reserve leafy
    tops and stalks for previous recipe)
1 tablespoon aniseed,
    dry roasted and ground (see note)
6 whole cloves
6 cloves garlic, peeled and crushed
1 tablespoon whole black peppercorns, cracked
2 teaspoons sea salt
2 cups (500ml/16fl oz) Jerez vinegar
1 cup (250ml/8fl oz) red wine vinegar
1 cup (150g/5oz) firmly packed dark brown sugar

Preheat oven to 180°C (350°F/Gas Mark 4).
  Line a baking dish with foil. Place washed
beetroot in dish, in one layer, and cover tightly
with foil. Roast 2 hours, or until tender when
pierced with a metal skewer.
  Remove beetroot from oven and cool in opened
foil in dish, until comfortable to handle. Slip off
skin and stalk ends. Cut beetroot into wedges and
pack into sterilised screw- or clip-top jars.
  Meanwhile, pound together aniseed, cloves,
garlic, peppercorns and salt in a mortar. Add
to remaining ingredients in a deep saucepan,
simmer uncovered for 30 minutes, or until
reduced by about one-third. Strain over beetroot,
releasing air bubbles with a metal spatula. Seal
jars. Refrigerate until required. Keeps well for
6-12 months.
SERVES 6-8

note: To dry roast aniseed, place it in a small
saucepan and shake over a moderate heat
until aromatic, or place in an oven tray and
roast for 15 minutes at 180°C (350°F/Gas
Mark 4). Cool before grinding.

Rustic Apple Cake

625g (1¼ lb) tart cooking apples
    (such as Granny Smith)
4 green cardamom pods
1 cup (250ml/8fl oz) sweet dessert wine
200g (6½oz) unsalted butter,
    at room temperature
½ cup (110g/3½oz) caster sugar
2 free-range eggs, at room temperature
2 cups (300g/10½oz) self-raising flour
1 teaspoon bicarbonate of soda
1 tablespoon caster sugar, extra
1 teaspoon ground cardamom

Slice apples into a deep saucepan. Crack the
cardamom pods so they split but remain intact.
Add to apples, with wine. Cover and simmer for
25 minutes, or until apples are soft. Beat to a
purée with a wooden spoon and then push purée
through a coarse sieve into a bowl. Cool
completely. Discard skin and cores.
  Preheat oven to 180°C (350°F/Gas Mark 4).
  Beat butter and sugar until pale and fluffy.
Add eggs, individually, beating well after each
addition. Stir in flour, sifted with bicarbonate
of soda, alternately with 1½ cups apple purée.
  Pour into a buttered and base-lined 18cm (7in)
spring-form pan. Sprinkle top with combined extra
sugar and cardamom. Bake 35-40 minutes, or
until cake tests done. Cool 10 minutes in tin, turn
out onto a wire rack and cool completely. Wrap in
waxed paper and then foil for transportation.
SERVES 6-8

kite flying

'But if I stopped holding
The string of my kite,
It would blow with the wind
For a day and a night.'

'WIND ON THE HILL' FROM *NOW WE ARE SIX* A.A. MILNE (1882-1956)

Prawn and Salmon Terrine
with Best Bread

1 stalk lemongrass, coarsely chopped
16 large green prawns, peeled and deveined
8 slices smoked salmon
300g (9½oz) smoked salmon off-cuts
500g (1 lb) fresh ricotta
60g (2oz) butter, melted
1 tablespoon Tabasco sauce
½ cup (125ml/4fl oz) verjuice
8 sheets gelatine, soaked in cold water
Finely grated rind of 1 medium lemon

Place lemongrass in a large saucepan with 5cm (2in) water. Bring to a simmer, then position prawns in a steamer basket or colander over water. Cover and steam about 10 minutes, or until prawns are opaque. Cool.

Line a 5-cup terrine or loaf tin with a strip of baking paper, overhanging both long edges (to aid removal of mixture from dish). Line terrine neatly with sliced salmon, reserving 2-3 slices to cover.

Purée salmon off-cuts, ricotta, butter and Tabasco in blender. Warm verjuice in a small saucepan and dissolve squeezed gelatine in this. Blend into salmon mixture, with lemon rind.

Lay half the prawns, lengthways, along base of terrine. Cover with half the salmon mixture, then remaining prawns in same manner. Cover with remaining salmon mixture and finish with reserved sliced salmon.

Cover with plastic wrap and refrigerate several hours, or until set. Transport in terrine, turn out onto a plate or board and serve with the best bread you can find, and celery sticks and witlof leaves, if you wish. Pack these in snap-lock plastic bags for transportation.

SERVES 6-8

Lemon and Cardamom Syrup Cakes

180g (6oz) butter, melted
½ cup (110g/3½oz) caster sugar
½ cup (125ml/4fl oz) honey
4 medium free-range eggs, at room
    temperature
1 tablespoon finely grated lemon rind
1 teaspoon bicarbonate of soda
2 cups (300g/10½oz) self-raising flour
60g (2oz) fine semolina
1 teaspoon ground cardamom
1 cup (250ml/8fl oz) cultured buttermilk

Syrup
½ cup (125ml/4fl oz) lemon juice
½ cup (110g/3½oz) caster sugar
4 green cardamom pods, barely crushed

Preheat oven to 180°C (350°F/Gas Mark 4).

Beat together butter, sugar and honey until thick and pale. Add eggs individually, beating well after each addition. Stir in lemon rind and then sifted dry ingredients, alternating with buttermilk. Start and finish with dry ingredients.

Butter 18 x ⅓ cup (90ml/3fl oz) moulds or muffin tins. Spoon mixture into these, to almost fill. Bake 20 minutes, or until golden and springy to touch.

Meanwhile, simmer syrup ingredients for 15-20 minutes. Turn out cakes onto a tray, spoon hot syrup over warm cakes. Cool before packing into a lidded container.

MAKES 18

note: The cakes keep well for 4–5 days in an airtight container. They are delicious if warmed through (in the microwave for 10 seconds each, or wrapped in foil, in a slow oven) before eating, especially if they are several days old.

Coffee and Bitter Chocolate Walnut Cake

150g (5oz) unsalted butter, at room
    temperature
½ cup (100g/3½oz) firm pack dark brown sugar
200g (6½oz) dark chocolate (70 per cent
    cocoa solids), melted and cooled
3 medium free-range eggs
1 cup (250ml/8fl oz) very strong cold
    espresso coffee
2 cups (300g/10oz) self-raising flour, sifted
1 cup (100g/3½oz) walnuts, crushed

Preheat oven to 160°C (325°F/Gas Mark 3).

Whisk butter with sugar, chocolate and eggs, until thick and smooth. Whisk in coffee, then stir in flour and walnuts.

Pour into a greased and base-lined 23cm (9in) spring-form pan (or two 18cm/7in pans). Bake for 40 minutes or until a metal skewer inserted into cake comes out clean.

Cool in tin, on a wire rack, for 20 minutes. Remove from tin and cool completely. Wrap cake in waxed paper and then foil for transportation.

Dust with pure cocoa powder before serving, with mascarpone or thick cream, if desired.

SERVES 6-8

Fresh Lemonade

2 cups (440g/1 lb) caster sugar
4 cups (1L/1¾ pints) water
Finely grated rind and juice of 10 large lemons
Iced soda or mineral water, to serve

Combine sugar and water in a saucepan. Heat until sugar has dissolved. Add rind and juice, remove from heat, then cool. Pour into bottles and refrigerate until required.

To serve, combine with soda or mineral water, to taste.

MAKES ABOUT 2L (3½ pints)

symphony under the stars

(D I N N E R)

'The wonder is, not that the field of stars is so vast,
but that man has measured it.'

THE GARDEN OF EPICURUS ANATOLE FRANCE (1844-1924)

Tomato Pesto Tart

2 sheets ready-rolled frozen puff pastry,
    thawed
½ cup (125ml/4fl oz) thin pesto
    (bought or home-made, see recipe p56)
4 large Roma tomatoes
½ cup (125ml/4fl oz) full-cream
    natural yoghurt
¼ cup (60ml/2fl oz) thick cream
3 large free-range eggs

Preheat oven to 200°C (400°F/Gas Mark 5).

Line a 20 x 28cm (8 x 11in) rectangle loose
bottom metal flan tin with pastry. Trim to size.

Spread pesto over base. Slice tomatoes
lengthways and arrange on pesto. Whisk
remaining ingredients until well combined.
Carefully pour around tomatoes (try to keep
tomatoes exposed).

Bake 30 minutes, or until filling at centre of tart
is firm to touch. Cool and transport in tin,
wrapped in a tea towel. Cut into slices to serve.

SERVES 6

Potato and Rosemary Bites

3 floury potatoes (about 750g), scrubbed
60g (2oz) butter
2 eschalots (about 100g/3½oz), peeled
¼ cup rosemary leaves
3 free-range eggs
1 egg yolk
100g (3½oz) chèvre
Salt and freshly ground black pepper
1 cup (150g/5oz) plain flour
1 cup fresh breadcrumbs
Light olive oil, for deep frying
Flaked sea salt, to serve

Cook potatoes in boiling salted water until tender,
about 20 minutes. Cool until easy to handle, then
peel. Mash with butter. Mince eschalots with
rosemary leaves in a food processor or grinder.
Stir into potato, with 1 egg and the yolk, and the
chèvre. Season with salt and black pepper to
taste. Refrigerate mixture for at least one hour.

Roll cold mixture into walnut-size balls, then roll
each in flour, dip in egg and roll in breadcrumbs.
Place on a tray lined with baking paper and
refrigerate until ready to fry.

Heat 7cm (3in) of oil in a deep pot. Fry potato
bites in batches. Remove with a slotted spoon and
drain on absorbent paper. When cool, pack into a
lidded container for transportation.

MAKES ABOUT 40

Prosciutto Wrapped Quail

6-9 quail
2 tablespoons ground sumac
2 tablespoons chopped fresh oregano
¼ cup (60ml/2fl oz) verjuice
18-27 thin slices prosciutto

Chop each quail into 2-4 pieces. Place in a bowl with sumac and chopped oregano. Turn pieces to coat. Cover and refrigerate as long as possible, or at least one hour. Sprinkle with verjuice. Wrap each piece of quail with prosciutto, then thread onto 6-9 pairs of metal or soaked bamboo skewers.

Preheat oven to 220°C (450°F/Gas Mark 6).

Lay skewers on rack in oven dish (or if dish is suitable size, suspend skewers from each end across width of dish).

Roast 30 minutes, turning and basting with juices after 15 minutes. Cool to room temperature. Wrap skewered quail in aluminium foil for transportation, or place in a suitable dish. Pack plenty of napkins—this is best as finger food.
SERVES 6

note: Sumac are purple berries found on a bush that grows wild in the Middle East and in parts of Italy. Sumac are usually sold ground as a dark reddish-coloured coarse powder, or in its dried-berry form. They have a sharp, fruity flavour. Ground sumac is available from Middle Eastern supermarkets and good delicatessens.

Watercress and Red Onion Salad with Walnut and Verjuice Dressing

1 bunch watercress
1 medium Spanish (red) onion
1 cup (250ml/8fl oz) walnut oil
1 cup (150g/5oz) walnut halves
1 tablespoon palm sugar, shaved or grated
½ cup (125ml/4fl oz) verjuice

Immerse watercress in a sink of cold water. Drain. Pick over cress, discarding any yellowing or damaged leaves and tough stalks.

Place watercress in a large snap-lock plastic bag. Peel and finely slice onion (a v-cutter or mandolin gives best results) and separate slices into rings. Place in bag with watercress. Seal and refrigerate until ready to pack picnic basket.

For dressing, heat oil in a small saucepan until moderately hot. Add nuts and cook until beginning to brown. Stir in sugar until dissolved. Remove from heat then carefully and slowly whisk in verjuice (it will spit if you add it too quickly). Cool mixture, then pour into a screw-top container for transportation.

Add to salad just before serving, either directly from bag, or you can pack a salad bowl and servers.

SERVES 6

Tangy Lime Pies

Pastry
1¼ cups (190g/6oz) flour
125g (4oz) unsalted butter
1 tablespoon icing sugar, sifted

Filling
1 egg, at room temperature
½ cup (60g/2oz) icing sugar
Finely grated rind and juice of 1 lime
60g (2oz) butter, melted
⅓ cup (50g/1½oz) ground almonds

For pastry, combine flour, butter and icing sugar in food processor or work with fingers until mixture clings together (add a few drops of lime juice if mixture is too dry). Shape into a flat disc, wrap in plastic and refrigerate 30 minutes.

Preheat oven to 190°C (375°F/Gas Mark 4). Roll pastry to 3mm (⅛in) thick and cut to fit 12 medium muffin tins. Freeze five minutes, prick bases and line each case with baking paper and cooking weights (or smaller paper baking cases filled with weights, or smaller metal tins).

Bake blind for 10 minutes. Remove paper and weights.

Reduce oven temperature to 160°C (325°F/Gas Mark 3).

Meanwhile, prepare filling. Whisk egg and sugar until light and fluffy. Add lime juice, butter and almonds. Beat well, until smooth. Stir in lime rind. Spoon into prepared cases to almost filled and cook 20 minutes, or until filling has set.

Remove from oven, cool, and transport in tins, wrapped in a tea towel, with a shaker of icing sugar to dust tarts before serving.

MAKES 12

under the trees

''Tis the time of year
When the young hot blood
Is swept in a life-tide
Up to a flood.'

SPRING DAME MARY GILMORE (1865-1962)

Continuous Sausage

1.5m (59in) thin sausage, in one piece
   (see note)
8 stalks rosemary, at least 10cm (4in) long
   (stripped of leaves except tip)
1 tablespoon olive oil

Form sausage into a flat coil, securing it as you
go by poking rosemary stalks into side of sausage,
to penetrate at least two rings of coil. Have the
leaves protruding out on either side of the coil.
Place between a hinged grill rack (or camping
toast rack—see note), brush with oil, then cook
over hot coals for 10 minutes on each side. Turn
onto a board, slice into wedges to serve.
SERVES 6

note: Ask your butcher to make you the
sausage without tying it into links. Choose
whatever flavour you prefer.

  Grill racks are usually hinged with two split
rings. If you find the grill is too tightly
hinged to accommodate the thickness of the
sausage, widen the distance by swapping the
split rings with larger ones, or simply secure
with thin wire.

Smoked Onion Relish

6 large red onions
½ cup (125ml/4fl oz) pomegranate molasses
1 tablespoon finely julienned lemon rind
1 tablespoon olive oil
4 whole cloves

Place 1 cup woodchips in water to soak (see note).
Heat barbecue. When coals are glowing red
sprinkle drained chips over them. Place whole,
unpeeled onions on rack of barbecue, cover
with lid and set vents at smallest opening.
Smoke onions for 30 minutes. Remove onions
and cool, then peel. Cut flesh into medium dice
and combine with remaining ingredients in
a deep saucepan. Cover and cook slowly for
30-40 minutes, or until mixture thickens.
  Spoon into sterilised jars, seal and store in
a cool, dark place, or use while warm.
MAKES 3 CUPS (750ml/1¼ pints)

note: Special woodchips for barbecues can be
bought from kitchen and barbecue shops.

  The onions can be smoked and peeled, then
refrigerated in a sealed container for up to
one week before continuing with the recipe.

Grilled Corn Cakes

1 cup (150g/5oz) self-raising flour
1 teaspoon salt
Kernels from 1 corn cob
1 cup (250ml/8fl oz) grated potato, excess
    moisture squeezed out
90g (3oz) butter
1 egg
¾ cup (190ml/6fl oz) milk
2 tablespoons chopped fresh tarragon
Oil and butter, for frying

Sift flour and salt into a bowl. Stir in corn and
potato. Melt butter in a mixing jug, whisk in egg
and milk. Stir into other ingredients until well
combined. Stir in tarragon. Heat 1 tablespoon
each of oil and butter in a heavy-based frying pan.
Make each corn cake from 2 tablespoons of
mixture, cooking on both sides until golden.
Stack on paper towels. Transfer to a napkin-lined
lidded container for transportation. When about
to eat, toast the corn cakes in wire rack over the
low embers of the barbecue. Serve with smoked
onion relish (see recipe p32) and purchased
pickled baby cucumbers.
MAKES ABOUT 25

note: Chopped chilli can be added to this
mixture. The cakes can also be made blini
size and passed as hors d'oeuvres with sweet
chilli dipping sauce. Another version is to
substitute a 420g (15oz) can of creamed
corn for the fresh kernels, 500g (1 lb) crab
meat for the potato and fresh coriander for
the tarragon.

Mango in Lime Syrup

4 limes
⅓ cup (75g/2½oz) caster sugar
12 mint leaves, finely sliced
4 firm, ripe mangoes

Combine finely julienned lime rind and the juice
with caster sugar in a small saucepan. Heat,
stirring, until sugar has dissolved. Cool, then stir
in sliced mint.
   Peel and thinly slice mangoes. Place in a bowl or
lidded container and pour syrup over. Refrigerate
until required.
   Serve with baked custards (see recipe following).
SERVES 6

Baked Custards

1 tablespoon butter, melted
6 teaspoons honey
1 cup (250ml/8fl oz) milk
¼ cup (60ml/2fl oz) pure cream
100g (3½oz) chèvre
3 free-range eggs, lightly whisked

Preheat oven to 160°C (325°F/Gas Mark 3).
   Brush insides of 6 x ⅓ cup (90ml/3fl oz) custard
cups or ramekins or espresso cups with melted
butter. Place 1 teaspoon of honey in the base of
each cup, then put them in a deep baking dish.
   Combine milk, cream and chèvre in a saucepan,
stir over medium heat until smooth. Do not boil
or the custard will curdle.
   Pour mixture into a large jug or pouring bowl.
Whisk in eggs. Fill custard cups with the mixture.
   Pour hot water into baking dish, so that it comes
⅓ up the sides of custard cups. Place in centre of
oven and bake 15-20 minutes, or until set. Transport
in cups, covered with plastic wrap. Serve at room
temperature, either in cups, or turned out. Serve
with Mango in Lime Syrup (see recipe above).
SERVES 6

Honey Fritters

2 cups (500ml/16fl oz) light olive oil

Thinly pared rind of 1 orange

1 tablespoon sesame seeds

1 tablespoon aniseed

4 cups (600g/1lb 3½oz) plain flour

1 tablespoon ground cinnamon

⅓ teaspoon salt

Finely grated rind 1 lemon

1⅔ cup (430ml/14fl oz) sweet white wine

1 cup cold water

1 cup (250ml/8fl oz) honey

Heat oil with rind and seeds in a deep saucepan, over a low heat, for about 10 minutes. Cool and then strain oil, discarding solids (see note).

Sift flour, cinnamon and salt into a mixing bowl. Stir in rind, wine and ⅔ cup water. Mix to combine, then knead into a ball. Roll on a lightly floured surface to no more than 3mm (⅛in) thick. Cut into diamonds.

Heat oil in a deep frying pan, until almost at smoking point.

Combine honey and remaining ⅓ cup (90ml/3fl oz) water in a saucepan and heat until simmering. Pour half into base of a serving plate. Fry fritters, in batches without crowding pan. Turn once and remove with a slotted spoon to serving plate. When all are cooked, pour remaining honey syrup over them. Pack into a lidded container for transportation.

MAKES 36

note: About 2 tablespoons of purchased pure orange oil, can be added to the light olive oil to flavour it, instead of infusing with rind.

in the courtyard

(L U N C H)

'All things that love the sun are out of doors.'

RESOLUTION AND INDEPENDENCE WILLIAM WORDSWORTH (1770-1850)

Smashed Chicken

2 large free-range chickens
4 lemons or 150g (5oz) preserved
    lemon pickle, to serve

Paste
2 small red chillies, chopped
    (remove seeds for less heat)
2 medium onions, peeled and quartered
1.5cm (2in) pieces of green ginger, peeled
2 roots coriander (roots, stems, leaves), chopped
2 cloves garlic, peeled
⅓ cup (90ml/3fl oz) lemon juice
2 tablespoons ghee
1 teaspoon ground cumin
1 teaspoon ground turmeric
½ teaspoon ground cloves
½ teaspoon ground cinnamon
½ teaspoon ground cardamom

Halve chickens lengthways. Trim excess fat and remove necks and giblets. Place chickens on work surface, cover with a clean tea towel and bash with a rolling pin to flatten (this ensures even grilling).

Process wet paste ingredients to an even texture in food processor or blender. Add spices and blend to combine. Spread mixture on both sides of each chicken piece. Place in a dish, cover and refrigerate for 2 hours or overnight. (The chicken could also be stored in large snap-lock plastic bags or plastic containers, if travelling to a barbecue site.)

Heat the barbecue until coals are glowing. Place chickens, skin side up, on grill for 20 minutes. Turn and cook skin side down for 15 minutes, or until juices run clear when thigh is pierced with a metal skewer or point of a knife.

Serve garnished with wedges of fresh lemon or preserved lemon pickle.

SERVES 8

Bean and Labna Salad

4 cardamom pods, barely crushed
450g (1 lb) mixed fresh beans (French beans,
    butter beans, flat Italian beans) trimmed
    and cut into 3cm (1½in) lengths
1 x 400g (14oz) can white beans, drained
16 Labna balls (see recipe p136)
    or baby bocconcini or balls of chèvre rolled
    in finely chopped herbs

Dressing
½ cup olive oil
    (use the oil from Labna if you wish)
½ cup white balsamic vinegar
¼ cup finely chopped fresh oregano
1 clove garlic, finely chopped

Half-fill a deep medium-sized saucepan with water. Add cardamom and bring to a boil. Add beans and simmer 5 minutes, then drain. Discard cardamom. Combine in a lidded container with canned white beans. When cool, stir through labna.

Combine dressing ingredients in a screw-top jar and shake. Pour over salad just before serving.

Smoked Tomato Sauce

6 large vine-ripened tomatoes
Fresh bay leaves, on branches
   (or use soaked or dried bay leaves)
1 cup chopped fresh oregano
3 eschalots (about 150g/5oz), finely chopped
½ cup (125ml/4fl oz) mustard seed oil

Heat barbecue. Soak 1 cup wood chips in water
(see note p32).

Score an 'X' in base of each tomato. When
coals are glowing red sprinkle drained chips over
them. Place tomatoes, core up, on a bed of bay
leaves. Cover barbecue with lid and set vents at
the smallest opening. Smoke tomatoes for
45 minutes.

Remove tomatoes from barbecue and cool on a
tray or in a dish in which the juices will collect.
Peel tomatoes and chop them roughly. Process
oregano, eschalots and mustard seed oil in a
blender until fairly smooth. Pour into a deep
frying pan and cook, stirring, over a medium heat
for 5 minutes. Add tomatoes and juices, cook
slowly, uncovered, for 20 minutes. Serve as is or
pour into sterilised bottles and seal until required.
Store refrigerated.

MAKES 2 CUPS

note: For a smooth sauce, blend mixture. It
will become thick and a dark orange colour,
and is better this way if used as a dip.

The tomatoes can be smoked and peeled,
then refrigerated in a sealed container for up
to 7 days before continuing with the recipe.
This is a good way to make use of the last
embers of a barbecue.

Mustard Potatoes

6-8 medium potatoes
2 tablespoons brown mustard seeds
¼ cup (60ml/2fl oz) mustard seed oil
2 eschalots, peeled and chopped

Wash potatoes, peel if you wish, then cut into
wedges. Steam until just tender.

Dry roast mustard seeds in a covered frying pan.
Add oil (see note p52) and heat then add
eschalots and stir until softening. Add steamed
potatoes, turn to coat and cook over medium-hot
heat for 20 minutes, until golden. Serve immediately.

SERVES 8

note: If travelling to a barbecue site, pack
steamed potato into a snap-lock plastic bag,
and roasted mustard with eschalots in another.

Passionfruit Amaretto Ice-cream

600ml (1 pint) pure cream
4 egg yolks
½ cup (110g/4oz) caster sugar
2 tablespoons Amaretto
⅔ cup (180ml/6fl oz) passionfruit pulp
    (about 6 passionfruit)

Beat cream with yolks and caster sugar until thick
and pale. Stir in Amaretto and passionfruit. Pour
into an ice-cream maker and churn according to
manufacturer's instructions. Spoon into a plastic
container and freeze until required. Alternatively,
pour into a shallow lidded freezer container and
freeze until sludgy. Stir with a fork to break up
any ice crystals, then freeze again until sludgy.
Repeat process three times before finally freezing.

Remove from freezer to refrigerator at least
30 minutes before serving, or if travelling to a
barbecue site, wrap ice-cream container in sheets
of newspaper and pack in cool-box with ice.
MAKES ABOUT 1L (1³/₄ pints)

Almond Meringues

½ cup (125ml/4fl oz) egg whites
    (4-6 eggs, depending on size)
1¼ cups (275g/9oz) caster sugar
1 teaspoon lemon juice
2 teaspoons pure icing sugar
½ cup (75g/3½oz) flaked almonds

Heat oven to 120°C (250°F/Gas Mark 1).
Line two flat baking trays with baking paper.
Combine egg whites, sugar, lemon juice and a
pinch of salt in bowl of an electric mixer and
whisk on high speed for 15 minutes. The mixture
should be stiff, glossy and smooth. Sift icing sugar
over mixture and, using a large metal spoon, fold
in. Use 2 dessertspoons to shape meringues. Take
a spoonful of mixture and using the other spoon,
push mixture into a mound on prepared tray.

Don't try to smooth the surface, simply leave
mixture as it is.

Space mounds at least 2.5cm (1in) apart.
Sprinkle each meringue with flaked almonds. Bake
for 1½ hours, then cool in oven with door ajar. The
meringues should remain quite white, with barely
a hint of colour. When quite cold, store in airtight
containers until required.
MAKES ABOUT 24

with cocktails

'Three o'clock is always too late or too early
for anything you want to do.'

NAUSEA JEAN-PAUL SARTRE (1905-1980)

Campari Cocktails

1 tablespoon Campari
1 tablespoon sweet vermouth
1 tablespoon gin
½ cup (125ml/4fl oz) crushed ice
3 thin slices orange
Soda water

Shake together the Campari, vermouth, gin and
ice. Place orange in a tall glass, pour mixture over
and top with chilled soda water.
MAKES 1 DRINK

Limoncella

750ml (27fl oz) vodka
Rind from 6 medium lemons
1 cup lemon balm sprigs, washed and dried
¾ cup (165g/5½oz) raw sugar
2 cups (500ml/16fl oz) water

Combine vodka, lemon rind and balm in a large
glass jar. Keep in a cool, dark place for 7 days.
  Combine sugar with water in a saucepan. Heat,
stirring, until sugar has dissolved. Boil 5 minutes,
cool. Strain vodka mixture into a clean container,
stir in syrup. Seal and store another 7 days. Pour
into sterilised bottles. Freeze at least 6 hours
before using. Transport in a cool-box. Drink neat
in shot glasses, or in small tumblers, over ice.
MAKES 1.25L (2 pints)

Toasted Smoked Trout Sandwiches

1 smoked trout
½ cup (125ml/4fl oz) good quality
    egg mayonnaise
8 anchovy fillets and 1 tablespoon of their oil
1 eschalot, peeled and chopped finely
2 tablespoons olive oil
1 long loaf Turkish bread
Watercress sprigs, for garnish

Skin and bone trout. Break up flesh into flakes.
Blend mayonnaise, anchovy fillets and eschalot
until fairly smooth. Transfer to a bowl and stir
in trout.
  Combine anchovy and olive oil. Cut loaf in half
through middle. Open it up and brush both inside
surfaces with oil. Place these on barbecue and
grill until just golden. Remove and spread the
trout mixture over toasted side of one of the
halves. Top with second half. Brush both outer
surfaces with oil, then place entire loaf in a
hinged grill rack. Position on barbecue and toast
on both sides.
  Turn onto a board and cut into 2.5cm (1in)
'fingers', with watercress sprigs as garnish.
SERVES 8

Spatchcock with Tapenade Mayonnaise

8 spatchcock

4 lemons

16 sprigs fresh oregano

½ cup (125ml/4fl oz) olive oil

4 cloves garlic, peeled

Tapenade Mayonnaise

4 egg yolks

¼ cup (60ml/2fl oz) lemon juice

¼ teaspoon chilli powder

1 cup (250ml/8fl oz) olive oil

½ cup (125ml/4fl oz) tapenade or purée ½ cup
(125g/4oz) stoned black olives

Wash spatchcock and pat dry. Halve lemons.
Squeeze a little juice from each half over a
spatchcock, then place a lemon half in the cavity
of each bird, with a sprig of oregano. Tie legs
together with kitchen string.

Purée remaining oregano with olive oil and
garlic, seasoned with salt and freshly ground
black pepper to taste. Pour mixture over birds,
cover and stand until required. (Refrigerate if
standing for more than 30 minutes.)

Heat barbecue until coals are glowing. Place
birds, back down, on rack. Cook 20 minutes, then
turn and cook breast side for 15 minutes. Cook
each leg side for 5 minutes.

To make mayonnaise, lightly whisk yolks with
lemon juice and chilli. Slowly whisk in oil, then
stir in tapenade.

Serve spatchcock warm or at room temperature
with Tapenade Mayonnaise passed separately.

SERVES 8

Grilled Mixed Asparagus

4 bunches asparagus (a mixture of purple,
white and green)

1 tablespoon olive oil

Snap off tough stalk ends of asparagus and trim
break to neaten. Roll spears in olive oil, then place
in a single layer on a hinged grill rack. Cook over
glowing coals for 2 minutes on each side.

SERVES 8

Quail Egg and Eschalot Salad

8 eschalots (shallots), peeled and sliced
into very thin rings

½ iceberg lettuce, shredded very finely

24 quail eggs, soft boiled and peeled

Dressing

2 tablespoons good quality egg mayonnaise

1 tablespoon Dijon or other creamy mustard

½ cup (125ml/4fl oz) verjuice

Combine eschalots and lettuce on a serving plate
or lidded container. Make a 'nest' for the eggs and
place them in it. Cover and refrigerate until
required.

Combine dressing ingredients in a screw-top jar
and shake well. When ready to serve, drizzle
dressing over salad.

SERVES 8

Pineapple in Palm Sugar with Crème Fraîche

1 sweet pineapple
125g (4oz) palm sugar, shaved or grated
300ml (½ pint) crème fraîche (or sour cream)

Cut top off pineapple then halve lengthways.
Remove skin and cut out eyes. Cut into 1cm (½in)
thick slices. Lay in a dish and sprinkle palm sugar
over top. Stand at room temperature until
required. The sugar will melt.

When ready, grill pineapple over hot coals,
to warm it through and caramelise the juices.
Turn once.

Serve immediately with crème fraîche.
SERVES 8

Brown Sugar Shortbread

125g (4oz) unsalted butter,
    at room temperature
90g (3oz) dark brown sugar
1 cup (150g/5oz) plain flour
1 teaspoon cinnamon

Preheat oven to 180˚C (350˚F/Gas Mark 4).

Beat butter with electric mixer until pale, add
brown sugar and beat until smooth. Stir in sifted
flour and cinnamon, until well combined. Roll into
walnut-sized balls and place on baking tray. Press
with the floured tines of a fork, to flatten slightly.
Bake 15 minutes. Cool on tray, then transfer to
a wire rack. Pack into a lidded container for
transportation.
MAKES 18

early evening

(D I N N E R)

'It is a beauteous evening, calm and free.'

IT IS A BEAUTEOUS EVENING WILLIAM WORDSWORTH (1770-1850)

Broad Bean and Garlic Purée with Charred Turkish Bread

500g (1 lb) shelled broad beans
  (or use frozen broad beans)
4 cloves roasted garlic and ¼ cup
  (60ml/2fl oz) of their oil (see recipe p118)
2 tablespoons verjuice
1 tablespoon lemon juice
Salt and freshly ground black pepper
1 loaf Turkish bread
½ cup (125ml/4fl oz) olive oil
3 tablespoons sumac (see note p30)

Cook beans in boiling water until tender. Cool, then peel. Discard skins.

Blend beans with garlic and oil, verjuice, lemon juice and season with salt and freshly ground black pepper to taste. Place in a lidded container for transportation.

Cut loaf of bread in half through middle. Open it up and brush both inside surfaces with oil then sprinkle with sumac. Place bread on barbecue and grill until just golden. Slice into fingers and serve with bean purée.

SERVES 8

Mesquite Roast Beef Rib with Honey Mustard

½ cup (125ml/4fl oz) honey
½ cup (125ml/4fl oz) Dijon mustard
1 beef standing rib roast (4-6 ribs)

Combine honey and mustard to a smooth paste. Spread evenly over beef. Place meat on a rack in a roasting pan, suitable for using on your barbecue. (If travelling to a barbecue site, place meat in a large plastic bag for transportation.)

Heat barbecue until coals are glowing red. Place roasting pan with beef on grill, pour water into roasting dish to just cover the base. Close lid of barbecue and roast meat for 1 hour. Remove from heat and stand 10 minutes before carving.

The meat will be medium-rare.

SERVES 8

Artichoke and Red Capsicum Salad

3 red capsicums (bell peppers)
3 yellow capsicums (bell peppers)
250g (8oz) artichokes in oil

Cut capsicums in half, remove seeds and pith and grill on barbecue, skin side down, until skin blackens and blisters (or grill in the oven, skin side up). Place capsicum in a bowl, cover with a plate and stand until cool enough to handle.

Peel and discard skin. Slice capsicum into 6mm (¼in) strips. Combine with any juices and the artichokes and oil. Place in a lidded container. Serve at room temperature.

SERVES 8

Crushed Bintje Potatoes with Parmesan

1kg (2lb) Bintje potatoes
(or other small, waxy potatoes)
½ cup (125ml/4fl oz) olive oil
½ cup (90g/3oz) finely grated Parmesan

Scrub potatoes and boil in skins until just tender. Cool until easy to handle, then peel.

Heat a non-stick or heavy-based frying pan. Add the oil and heat a little, then add potatoes. Crush them with a potato masher to form a flat cake. Fry until base is golden. Sprinkle with Parmesan and place under hot grill briefly.

Serve in wedges.

SERVES 8

note: Duck fat is a wonderful frying medium for this recipe. It can be bought canned.

To extend this recipe add anchovies, fresh herbs, roasted garlic or even cubed haloumi cheese.

Latte Jellies and Clotted Cream

8 leaves gelatine
4 tablespoons dark brown sugar
2 cups (500ml/16fl oz) espresso coffee
2 cups full-cream milk
Clotted or pure thick cream, to serve

Soak gelatine in cold water for 5 minutes.

Dissolve sugar into hot coffee. Squeeze gelatine to remove excess water, then stir into coffee until dissolved. Stir in cold milk. Pour into 8 x ½ cup (125ml/4fl oz) moulds or glasses and cool at room temperature, then refrigerate until set. Either unmould or serve in glasses, accompanied by clotted or pure thick cream. Transport in moulds or glasses.

SERVES 8

boating

barefoot on the deck (breakfast)

rafting up (lunch)

escape in the dinghy (afternoon tea)

dusk on the water (dinner)

by the light of the moon (supper)

~

riding

back packed (morning tea)

in the shade (lunch)

tiffin time (late lunch)

catching butterflies (afternoon tea)

summer

barefoot on the deck

(B R E A K F A S T)

'For it's Mornin'! Mornin'! The leaves are all ashine:
There's treasure all about the place; an' all of it is mine.'

'A MORNING SONG' FROM *JIM OF THE HILLS* C.J. DENNIS (1876-1938)

Cinnamon Poached Peaches

4 cinnamon sticks
1 medium lemon, sliced thinly
1 cup (220g/7oz) raw sugar
3 cups (750ml/25fl oz) water
12 firm, ripe yellow peaches

Combine cinnamon, lemon and sugar in a deep pan. Add water and simmer until sugar is dissolved.

Add peaches, turning them to coat with syrup. Cover, then poach peaches in gently simmering syrup for 20 minutes. Turn peaches occasionally during the cooking time.

Spoon into a clip- or screw-top jar. Pour syrup over. Seal.
SERVES 6

note: Freeze leftover syrup and use again for poaching other fruit. I do this several times with poaching syrup; the result is an increasingly intense and complex delicious flavour. For a special sauce, reduce such 'layer-upon-layer' syrup by boiling until thick and sticky. Add intensity to cakes by using 'layered' syrup as part of the liquid content.

Honeycomb Yoghurt

125g (4oz) honeycomb
2 cups (500ml/16fl oz) mild natural yoghurt

Just before required, cut honeycomb into 1cm (½in) dice and combine with yoghurt in a bowl. Pass separately with Cinnamon Poached Peaches (see recipe opposite).
SERVES 6

Bacon and Sourdough Sandwiches with Lemon Walnut Mayonnaise

250g smoked short bacon rashers, thick cut
12 thick slices sourdough bread
½ cup (125ml/4fl oz) Lemon Walnut
    Mayonnaise (see recipe below)
1 firm, ripe avocado, sliced

Grill bacon until beginning to crisp. (If facilities on the boat are insufficient, grill the bacon at home and pack wrapped in paper towels, in a sealed plastic container. Use either at room temperature or warm in oven.)

If you have the facilities, grill one side of each slice of bread, otherwise use as is.

Spread ungrilled side of the bread generously with Lemon Walnut Mayonnaise. Place bacon on six of the slices, top with avocado and then the remaining bread.

SERVES 6

Lemon Walnut Mayonnaise

6 egg yolks
1 tablespoon lemon juice
2 tablespoons finely grated lemon rind
Pinch of salt
1 cup (250ml/8fl oz) walnut oil

Whisk yolks with lemon juice and rind and salt. Very slowly whisk in walnut oil, adding it in a slow, steady stream, to give a smooth, thick mayonnaise.

MAKES 1½ CUPS (375ml/12fl oz)

note: For a simple variation use mustard seed oil (taste first and if yours is a strongly flavoured variety, you may wish to dilute it with olive oil).

Sweet Walnut Bread

3 large free-range eggs
1 cup (250ml/8fl oz) milk
1 teaspoon vanilla essence
2½ cups (375g/12oz) self-raising flour
½ cup (75g/2½oz) coconut milk powder
2 teaspoons ground cinnamon
1 cup (225g/7oz) raw caster sugar
1 cup (125g/4oz) chopped walnuts
90g (3oz) butter, melted

Preheat oven to 180°C (350°F/Gas Mark 4). Grease a 6-cup (17cm x 10cm x 9cm/7in x 4in x 3½in) loaf tin with butter. Line the base with baking paper.

Whisk eggs with milk and vanilla. Sift flour, coconut milk powder and cinnamon into a bowl. Stir in caster sugar and walnuts.

Stir butter into egg mixture. Make a well in centre of dry ingredients, add liquid and mix until just combined.

Pour into prepared tin and cook in centre of oven for 1 hour or until a metal skewer inserted into bread comes out clean. Cool 5 minutes in tin, then turn out onto a wire rack to cool. Either transport in tin or wrap in waxed paper and then foil. Serve sliced thickly as is, or toasted and spread with butter.

MAKES 1 LOAF

rafting up

(L U N C H)

'There is nothing—absolutely nothing—half so much worth doing as simply messing about in boats'.

THE WIND IN THE WILLOWS KENNETH GRAHAME (1859-1932)

Ginger and Lime Drinks

500g (1 lb) fresh green ginger
⅓ cup (90ml/3fl oz) mild honey
2 cups (500ml/16fl oz) fresh lime juice
Mineral or soda water, to serve

To extract ginger juice, finely chop unpeeled ginger in a food processor or grate it. Spoon batches of about ½ cup (100g/3½oz) in centre of a double thickness piece of muslin, which is large enough to wrap the ginger in a pouch. Twist ends of muslin to squeeze ginger and extract juice into a bowl. Repeat until all ginger is squeezed and you have about ⅔ cup (180ml/6fl oz) juice (see note). Stand about 30 minutes (white sediment will settle into base of bowl). Pour juice into a clip-top bottle, large enough to accommodate honey and lime juice. Add these and shake to combine. Serve in glasses with ice and chilled mineral or soda water to taste.
MAKES 3 CUPS OF CONCENTRATE

note: Spoon the squeezed, chopped or grated ginger into sterilised glass jars, top with sherry and store for use in other cooking such as stir-fries and marinades, and for Lychees in Ginger and Lime Syrup (see recipe p64).

Chicken Parcels

Pancakes

1 cup (150g/5oz) plain flour
1 teaspoon seaweed salt
2 large free-range eggs
1¼ cup (310ml/10fl oz) milk
Butter for pan

Filling

500g (1 lb) chicken mince
3 eschalots or shallots (about 120g/4oz)
   minced or very finely chopped
   (or use green onion)
2 teaspoons seaweed salt (see note)
2 large free-range eggs, beaten
1 cup (50g/1½oz) fresh breadcrumbs
½ cup (90g/3oz) finely grated Parmesan
   or pecorino cheese
½ cup (75g/2½oz) plain flour
Vegetable oil for shallow frying

To make pancakes, combine flour and seaweed salt. Whisk in eggs and milk, to give a smooth pouring batter. Heat and then lightly grease a large (30cm) heavy-based frying pan (non-stick is ideal) with butter. Pour in enough batter to spread in a thin layer over entire base (tilt pan as you pour in batter). Cook until underside is golden and top set. Flip and cook briefly on topside. Turn out of pan and stack on work surface or on clean tea towel. Make 6 pancakes.

To prepare filling, combine mince, eschalots and seaweed salt. Divide into six portions and wrap each in a pancake, to form a long roll with ends tucked in.

Whisk eggs in a shallow dish. Place combined breadcrumbs and grated cheese in a similar dish and flour in another.

Lay a pancake roll in dish of flour, turn it to coat evenly, including ends. Tap off excess flour and coat pancake roll with egg, then evenly coat with breadcrumb mixture. Place crumbed roll on a tray, joined side down. Repeat with remaining rolls. Refrigerate until ready to fry.

Heat vegetable oil (about 8cm/3in deep) in a deep, wide saucepan, over a medium heat. Add rolls, one or two at a time, and fry about 8 minutes, turning twice, until evenly cooked to a deep golden brown. Remove with tongs and place on a tray lined with paper towels. When cold, pack into a carrying container. Serve at room temperature, sliced diagonally.
SERVES 6

note: Seaweed salt is a blend of sea salt and finely ground seaweeds. It is available from specialty food shops and delicatessens.

Potato, Bocconcini and Basil Salad

750g (1½ lb) Kipfler or other small,
   buttery potatoes
200g (6½oz) cherry bocconcini
½ cup (125ml/4fl oz) thin pesto
   (see recipe below)

Scrub and steam potatoes. Cool until easy to handle, peel if you wish. Combine with bocconcini and pesto, to serve.
SERVES 6

Thin Pesto

2 cups (100g/3½oz) basil leaves
½ cup (125ml/4fl oz) strained lemon juice
2 cloves garlic
2 tablespoons finely grated Parmesan
   or pecorino cheese
1 cup (250ml/8fl oz) walnut (or olive) oil

Combine ingredients in a blender and purée until smooth. Season with salt and freshly ground black pepper to taste. Store in a sealed jar.
MAKES ABOUT 2 CUPS

Lime Buttermilk Cake

2 tablespoons lime juice

2 tablespoons caster sugar

¾ cup (165g/5½oz) caster sugar

125g (4oz) unsalted butter, melted

3 large free-range eggs, at room temperature

½ cup (125ml/4fl oz) cultured buttermilk

1 cup (110g/3½oz) almond meal

½ cup (75g/2½oz) plain flour

1½ cups (225g/7oz) self-raising flour

20 sugared lime slices (recipe follows) or use
    finely sliced limes tossed in caster sugar

Preheat oven to 180°C (350°F/Gas Mark 4).

Combine lime juice and 2 tablespoons of sugar in a pan, heat to dissolve sugar, then cool. Whisk butter, lime syrup, remaining sugar, eggs and buttermilk until combined, about 3 minutes. Stir in almond meal and sifted flours until smooth.

Pour into a 23cm (9in) round, 5cm (2in) deep paper cake case (see note). Arrange lime slices in a decorative pattern on top.

Bake 45 minutes, or until a metal skewer inserted into cake comes out clean. Cool and transport in case.

SERVES 6-10

note: Paper cake cases are available from some specialist kitchenware and cooking shops. They are made in almost all the standard cake tin shapes. They are especially suitable for transporting, as the cake can be sliced through the paper case, and the case discarded when used. If they are unavailable in your area, simply substitute a conventional cake tin of the same size.

Sugared Lime Slices

This is an easy way to preserve in-season limes for use in sweet recipes throughout the year.

Thinly slice limes, layering them in small jars (about the diameter of the limes), with caster sugar sprinkled generously between each layer. Secure lids tightly, turn jars upside down and stand on lid for 24 hours. Repeat, turning daily for 1 week. By this time the sugar will have dissolved and there will be a quantity of syrup in the jar. Store in a cool dark place for up to 12 months. Refrigerate once opened.

escape in the dinghy

(AFTERNOON TEA)

'Summer afternoon—summer afternoon; to me those have always been the two most beautiful words in the English language.'

A BACKWARD GLANCE EDITH WHARTON (1861-1937) QUOTING HENRY JAMES

**Salmon Cream with Roe
and Mini Pappadums**

6 sheets gelatine

⅔ cup (160ml/5fl oz) lemon juice

600ml (1 pint) sour cream

300g (10½oz) smoked salmon (off-cuts
   are suitable)

1 tablespoon Tabasco

½ cup (30g/1oz) fresh dill tips

100g (3½oz) salmon roe

50g (1½oz) red chilli mini pappadums

1 cup (250ml/8fl oz) vegetable oil

To make the salmon cream with roe, soak gelatine in cold water for 10 minutes. Heat lemon juice in a small saucepan. Squeeze out gelatine and stir into lemon juice, until dissolved. Cool liquid slightly.

Combine sour cream, smoked salmon, Tabasco and lemon mixture in a blender or food processor and blend until smooth. Stir in dill and roe. Pour into moulds, cover and refrigerate until set. Transport in mould. Makes 4 cups.

To cook mini pappadums, heat vegetable oil in a deep pan. Test one pappadum. Drop it into the oil—if it immediately rises to the surface the oil is hot enough. Cook in batches, removing from oil as soon as they rise. Drain on paper towels. Store in an airtight container for 2-3 days.

SERVES 2

note: For a low-fat version, cook pappadums in a single layer in the microwave, leaving the centre of the plate empty. Usually 20 seconds on high is sufficient, but experiment with your microwave for the correct timing.

Seaweed Crackers

1 cup (150g/5oz) plain flour
1 tablespoon seaweed salt
2 tablespoons strained lemon juice
2 tablespoons vegetable oil
1 cup shredded toasted nori

Combine flour and salt. Stir in combined liquids
to make a crumbly dough (you may need to add
a few drops of chilled water). Knead into a ball,
flatten into a disc. Wrap in plastic and refrigerate
20 minutes.

Preheat oven to 180°C (350°F/Gas Mark 4).

Break dough into two pieces. Roll each through
the widest setting of a pasta machine (see note) to
make a smooth sheet. You may need to patch the
dough and roll at this setting 2-3 times before it
holds together well. Spread some of the nori over
sheet of dough, fold dough in half to enclose nori,
and then pass this piece through pasta machine,
still on widest setting. Gradually roll dough
through all settings, finishing with the narrowest.
Lay sheet of dough on work surface and cut into
2.5cm (1in) wide ribbons, across the width of the
sheet. Place these on a lightly greased or non-stick
baking tray and bake in centre of oven for 8-10
minutes, or until beginning to brown on edges.
Cool 1 minute on tray, then transfer to a wire rack
to cool completely. Store in an airtight container
for transportation. Will keep well for one week.
Serve with salmon cream (see recipe opposite).
SERVES 2

note: If you don't have a pasta machine, use
a rolling pin and roll the dough between two
sheets of baking paper as thinly as possible.

Orange, Fig and Halva Bites

12 white Greek figs
1 cup (250ml/8fl oz) orange juice
2 tablespoons finely julienned orange rind
150g (5oz) vanilla halva (see note)

Using a small, sharp pointed knife, make a small
incision in the side of each fig. Place figs and
juice in a shallow dish and stand 2 hours, or
until figs are softening. Pour figs and juice into
a small saucepan and cook over a low heat for
20 minutes. The figs should retain their shape
but have plumped and softened considerably.
Pour into a shallow dish and stand until cool.

Mix orange rind into halva to give a smooth
paste. Stuff a teaspoonful of this mixture into
each fig, reforming the fig and pressing cut edges
together. Pack into a small lidded container and
refrigerate until required. Serve whole or sliced
with coffee.
MAKES 12 PIECES

note: Halva is a confection of ground
sesame seeds, honey and halva root (an
extract from the root of a Mediterranean
tree), which gives halva its light, crunchy
texture. It is available from good
delicatessens.

dusk on the water

(DINNER)

'A loaf of bread,' the Walrus said,
'Is what we chiefly need:
Pepper and vinegar besides
Are very good indeed—
Now, if you're ready, Oysters dear,
We can begin to feed.'

THE WALRUS AND THE CARPENTER LEWIS CARROLL (1832-1898)

Oysters with Grilled Bread, Balsamic Vinegar and Seaweed Salt

6 freshly shucked oysters per person
1 loaf Turkish bread, grilled until golden
    and cut into thin slices
White balsamic vinegar
Seaweed salt

Present oysters with small containers of salt and vinegar and some bread on each plate. Provide small skewers or toothpicks for lifting oysters from shells.

Smoked Trout Nicoise

3 smoked trout
500g (1 lb) flat green beans, trimmed and
    cut into 5cm (2in) lengths, blanched
6-9 small new potatoes, steamed
24 quail eggs, soft boiled
1 cup (175g/5½oz) black olives
6-9 anchovy fillets
Lemon Walnut Mayonnaise (see recipe p52)

The ingredients for this salad can be prepared at home and then transported prior to assembly.

Remove skin from trout and lift flesh, in as large pieces as possible, off the bones. Wrap in waxed paper and place in a plastic lidded container for transportation. Pack remaining ingredients into separate snap-lock plastic bags for transportation.

To assemble, combine beans and quartered potatoes in a serving dish. Add trout, broken into chunks. Peel and add halved eggs. Add olives and then scatter anchovies over top. Pour over a little Lemon Walnut Mayonnaise to serve, passing remainder separately.

SERVES 6

Lychees in Ginger and Lime Syrup

½ cup (110g/3½oz) raw caster sugar
½ cup (125ml/4fl oz) fresh strained lime juice
Finely julienned rind from 3 limes
1 teaspoon chopped ginger (see recipe p55)
    or grated green ginger
1kg (2 lb) lychees, peeled (see note)

Combine sugar, lime juice, rind and ginger in
a small saucepan and heat until simmering and
sugar has dissolved.

  Place peeled lychees in a lidded container, pour
hot syrup over and stir to mix. Cover and
refrigerate until required.

  Serve with Saffron and Pistachio Rice Puddings
(see recipe opposite) or as a breakfast fruit.
SERVE 6-10

note: The easiest way to peel a lychee is to
remove a small circle of skin from the base
end of fruit, exposing the flesh. Simply
squeeze lychee with thumb and forefinger at
stem end, and the intact fruit will pop out.
This is especially effective when you are
eating as you peel, and the lychee is squeezed
directly into your mouth.

Saffron and Pistachio Rice Puddings

1 cup (200g/6½oz) shortgrain rice
    or sushi rice
1 teaspoon saffron threads
3½ cups (875ml/1 pint 9fl oz) milk
1 tablespoon Jerez sherry
1 teaspoon orange flower water
2 tablespoons honey
    (orange blossom is good if you can get it)
½ cup (75g/2½oz) pistachio kernels, roasted

Line 6 x ¾ cup (165ml/5½fl oz) moulds with a
double thickness of damp muslin, leaving enough
overhang to fold over top of filled mould. Combine
all ingredients except pistachios in a deep
saucepan. Cook over a medium heat, uncovered,
for 25 minutes, stirring frequently. Stand off the
heat 10 minutes (all liquid should be absorbed),
then stir in pistachios.

  Spoon warm mixture into moulds, packing it
down with the back of a spoon. Bring up edges
of muslin and fold over top of filling in moulds.
Refrigerate overnight. Transport to boat, in
moulds, packed in a lidded container. Serve at
room temperature, turned out onto a plate, with
lychees and some of the ginger syrup spooned
over rice.
SERVES 6

by the light of the moon

'They dined on mince, and slices of quince,
Which they ate with a runcible spoon.'

THE OWL AND THE PUSSYCAT EDWARD LEAR (1812-1888)

Peach Paste

2kg (4 lb) ripe firm yellow peaches,
    washed, quartered and stones discarded
½ cup (125ml/4fl oz) strained lemon juice
2 cups (550ml/16fl oz) cold water
1.5kg (3 lb) raw sugar
1 x 50g (2½oz) packet Jamsetta
    (a manufactured dry pectin available
    from delicatessens and cooking shops)

Combine yellow peaches, lemon juice and water
in a large deep pot. Cover, bring to a simmer and
cook 15-20 minutes, until peaches are soft and
breaking up. Purée peaches in pan using an
electric processing wand, or transfer mixture to
a blender, purée and return to pan. Add combined
sugar and Jamsetta and stir until sugar has
dissolved. Cook over a medium heat, stirring
frequently, until mixture is very thick and a
teaspoonful sets when dropped onto a cold
saucer (about 30 minutes). Spoon or pour into
shallow moulds lined with baking paper
(lamington tins, small loaf tins, flan dishes are all
suitable). Cool, then stand, uncovered, in a warm
position for 1 week. If you have a sheltered sunny
outdoor spot, leave the trays there during the
day, covered with muslin. The mixture will
condense and become firm enough to cut easily.
  Wrap uncut blocks in waxed paper and then
plastic, or place in an airtight container.

Refrigerate until required. The paste will keep
for 9-12 months if stored correctly. Serve with
cheeses and biscuits.
MAKES ABOUT 5 CUPS

note: Peach paste (and quince paste) can be
used to enhance the flavour of fruit poaching
syrups, chopped up into cake mixtures,
melted and used as a glaze for meat, warmed
and spread over the base of pastry cases for
sweet tarts or used mixed with nuts to stuff
into the centre of baked apples or pears. The
possibilities go on.

Oat Biscuits

50g (1½oz) rolled oats,
   ground in a nut grinder until very fine
1¼ cups (175g/5½oz) organic bakers flour
   (unbleached bread flour)
1 teaspoon baking powder
1 tablespoon dark brown sugar
150g (5oz) butter, at room temperature

Combine ingredients in a food processor or
electric mixer and work to stiff dough.
   Shape into a disc, wrap and refrigerate for
30 minutes.
   Preheat oven to 180°C (350°F/Gas Mark 4).
   Roll dough between two sheets of baking paper
to 3mm (⅛in) thick, then cut into rounds with a
5cm (2in) fluted biscuit cutter. Transfer to a lightly
greased or non-stick baking tray. Prick each
biscuit in centre with a fork. Bake for 12-15
minutes, until barely colouring on edges. Cool
5 minutes on trays, then transfer to a wire rack
to cool completely. Store in an airtight container.
MAKES 28

Kolonji Crackers

1¾ cups (170g/5½oz) grated cheddar
1 cup (150g/5oz) finely grated Parmesan
1½ cups (225g/7oz) plain flour
155g (5oz) cold butter, diced
2 teaspoons ground cardamom
2 teaspoons kolonji seeds
   (also known as Nigella seeds and
   erroneously as black cumin seeds)

Combine ingredients in a food processor or
electric mixer and process until the mixture
resembles coarse breadcrumbs. Add a few drops
of chilled water if necessary. Form dough into
a disc. Wrap and refrigerate up to 1 hour.
   Preheat oven to 200°C (400°F/Gas Mark 5).
   Cut dough into 1cm (½in) wide strips. Roll each
into a snake, place this between two sheets of
baking paper and then flatten it as thinly as
possible with a rolling pin. Using a metal spatula,
lift 5cm (2in) long pieces off the strip (the edges
will be ragged) and place on a lightly greased or
non-stick baking tray. Bake for 4-6 minutes, until
golden. Cool slightly on tray, then transfer to a
wire rack to cool completely. Store in an airtight
container. The crackers will keep for up to a week.
   Overall quantity depends on the size you make
the crackers.

Chocolate Pecan Pie

Pastry
125g (4oz) unsalted butter
1¼ cups (190g/6oz) plain flour
¾ teaspoon salt

Filling
2 large free-range eggs
1 cup (220g/7oz) caster sugar
60g (2oz) plain flour
125g (4oz) butter, melted
1 cup (175g/5½oz) chocolate chips
1 cup (115g/3½oz) coarsely chopped
    pecan nuts
1 tablespoon whisky
1 teaspoon vanilla essence
Icing sugar, for dusting
Thick cream, to serve

To make pastry, using two knives, cut butter into flour and salt in a mixing bowl, until mixture resembles coarse breadcrumbs. Stir in iced water, 1 tablespoon at a time, until mixture begins to cling together. Press into a ball. Wrap in plastic and chill 30 minutes.

Preheat oven to 180°C (350°F/Gas Mark 4).

Roll pastry to line a 23cm (9in) pie plate. Trim edges and crimp or score decoratively with a fork. Prick base, then chill 15 minutes.

For filling, whisk eggs until pale and frothy. Gradually whisk in sugar, then fold in sifted flour and butter. Stir in chocolate chips and nuts, then whisky and vanilla. Pour into pie shell and bake 40 minutes, or until pastry is golden and filling firm to touch in centre.

Cool pie to room temperature, then wrap and refrigerate for transportation. The pie is best eaten warm, if you have the facilities on the boat, but is also delicious cold. Dust with icing sugar and serve with thick cream.

SERVES 6

back packed

(M O R N I N G   T E A)

'Summertime, and the livin' is easy...'

PORGY AND BESS GEORGE GERSHWIN (1898-1937)

**Cinnamon Pikelets
with Blackberries and Cream**

1 cup (150g/5oz) self-raising flour
1 tablespoon ground cinnamon
⅓ cup (75g/2½oz) vanilla sugar
⅔ cup (170ml/5½fl oz) milk
1 egg
Butter for pan
Blackberries and thick cream, to serve
Cinnamon sugar, to serve

To make pikelets, sift dry ingredients into a mixing bowl. Make a well in centre and stir in combined milk and egg, to give a smooth batter. Stand for 10 minutes.

Heat a griddle or heavy-based large frying pan over a medium heat. Rub a little butter over surface (use a pastry brush or a scrunched up piece of baking paper) and then, using a large tablespoon, spoon mixture onto heated surface. Cook until bubbles appear on the surface and before they pop, flip pikelets and cook the other side until golden. Remove from pan and stack, wrapped in a clean tea towel (kitchen cloth), while cooking remaining mixture. Stack cool pikelets and wrap in waxed paper. Place in a carrying container with small pots of blackberries and thick cream. Take a shaker of cinnamon sugar, if you wish.
MAKES ABOUT 20

Spiced Pistachio Honey Bites

3 sheets filo pastry
150g (5oz) butter, melted
4 cups (500g/1 lb) pistachio kernels,
    coarsely chopped
1 cup (200g/6½oz) firmly packed
    dark brown sugar
1 tablespoon ground cinnamon
1 teaspoon freshly grated nutmeg
1 tablespoon ground cardamom
½ cup (125ml/4fl oz) honey
1 tablespoon rosewater
½ cup (60g/2oz) pistachio kernels, extra,
    for decoration

Preheat oven to 180°C (350°F/Gas Mark 4).

Brush each sheet of filo with some of the butter, you should have ½ cup (125ml/4fl oz) left for the recipe. Lay filo pastry in a 27 x 17½ x 3cm (10½ x 7 x 1¼in) baking tin, to cover base only.

Combine remaining ingredients (except extra pistachios) in a large mixing bowl and stir until thoroughly combined. Spoon into baking tin on top of filo and press down until mixture is firmly packed in.

Cut each extra kernel in half down its length and arrange in a decorative pattern on top of mixture, pressing down on each piece to secure.

Place in centre of oven and cook 20-25 minutes (if mixture begins to bubble up at edges, reduce oven temperature to 160°C (325°F/Gas Mark 3) for last 5 minutes. Cool in tin, then cut into small bites. The bites will keep very well, refrigerated, for 2 weeks, although you will probably have to hide them in the back of the fridge! If only using a small portion, keep remainder uncut until required. Pack into a lidded container for transportation.

MAKES ABOUT 40 PIECES

Apricot Tarts with Chèvre

1½ sheets ready-rolled frozen puff pastry
45g (1½oz) peach paste (see recipe p67)
45g (1½ oz) chèvre
1 tablespoon cream
6 small ripe apricots or plumcots
    (a cross between an apricot and plum,
    with a dark pink skin)
Icing sugar, for dusting

Preheat oven to 190°C (375°F/Gas Mark 4).

Lightly brush a 12-hole 5cm (2in) muffin tray with butter or spray with oil.

Semi thaw pastry (it is easier to handle than when completely soft) and using a 7½cm (3in) fluted biscuit cutter, cut 12 rounds. Position each over a hole on the tray, then gently ease in to fit.

Combine peach paste, chèvre and cream. Mash with a fork. Place a teaspoonful of the mixture in each pastry case. Halve and stone apricots, then place halves, skin side up, in each of the cases.

Cook tarts for 15 minutes, reduce the heat to 180°C (350°F/Gas Mark 4) and cook a further 5 minutes, or until pastry is golden. Cool slightly in tins, then remove to a wire rack to cool completely. Dust with icing sugar. Stack into a lidded container, separating layers with waxed paper. The tarts are best eaten the same day.
MAKES 12

in the shade

(L U N C H)

'Here with a Loaf of Bread beneath the bough,
A Flask of Wine, a book of Verse—and Thou'

THE RUBAIYAT OF OMAR KHAYYAM TRANS. EDWARD FITZGERALD (1809-1883)

Tuna and Potato Pots

750g (1½ lb) floury potatoes
½ cup (75g/2½oz) minced eschalots (shallots)
½ cup (125ml/4fl oz) good quality
　egg mayonnaise (or Lemon Walnut
　Mayonnaise, see recipe p52)
½ cup chopped fresh tarragon
425g (13½oz) can tuna in oil
8 anchovy fillets, mashed
3 tablespoons tapenade (black olive paste)
16-20 baby spinach leaves

Scrub potatoes and then boil in skins until tender, about 30 minutes. Drain and cool until comfortable to handle. Peel, then mash while warm with eschalots and mayonnaise. Stir in tarragon.

　Drain tuna and using a fork, flake the fish. Stir into potato with anchovies and tapenade.

Blanch spinach by dunking in a pot of simmering water, then immediately removing them with a wire scoop or large perforated spoon. Place leaves in a single layer on a clean tea towel (kitchen cloth) to absorb excess moisture. Trim any stalks from leaves.

　Line 4 x 1 cup (250ml/8fl oz) paper or ceramic moulds or a 4-cup (1L) loaf tin with spinach leaves, then spoon potato mixture in, pressing firmly to pack it down. Cover with plastic and refrigerate several hours or overnight. Transport in moulds and turn out to serve on a napkin. These are firm enough to be eaten from the hand.
MAKES 4

Cucumber, Tomato and Red Onion Salad with White Balsamic Vinegar

4 Lebanese cucumbers
4 medium vine-ripened tomatoes
1 small red (Spanish) onion, peeled
½ cup (125ml/4fl oz) white balsamic vinegar
　(or verjuice)

Wash and thinly slice cucumbers, tomatoes and onion. Place in layers in a lidded carrying container, which is just large enough to snugly fit salad. Season with salt and freshly ground black pepper to taste. Sprinkle with about 1 tablespoon of the vinegar, and pour remainder into a small bottle for transportation. Add this to salad just before serving.
SERVES 4

Peachy Cake

125g (4oz) unsalted butter,
    at room temperature
1 cup (220g/7oz) firm packed
    dark brown sugar
4 large free-range eggs
¼ cup (60ml/2fl oz) natural plain yoghurt
2 cups (500ml/16fl oz) peach purée (see
    recipe opposite)
3 cups (450g/14oz) self-raising flour
¼ cup (60g/2oz) dark brown sugar, extra,
    for topping

Preheat oven to 180°C (350°F/Gas Mark 4).
    Cream butter and sugar, then add eggs
individually, beating well after each addition.
    Stir in yoghurt and peach purée, then sifted
flour, until mixture is smooth.
    Pour into two 6-cup (1.5L/2½ pint) ring paper
cake baking cases or baking tins.
    Sprinkle tops with extra sugar.
    Bake 40-50 minutes, or until a metal skewer
inserted into cake comes out clean. Cool and
transport in baking case or tin. Serve with
extra peach purée passed separately. The cakes
freeze very well, and are also delicious when
warmed a little.
EACH CAKE SERVES 8

Peach Purée

1kg (2 lb) yellow peaches, stoned
Juice 1 medium lemon
1 tablespoon orange flower water
¼ cup (60ml/2fl oz) honey

Place all ingredients in a deep saucepan and cook
over a low heat, covered, for 20 minutes, or until
mushy. Purée in pan using a food processing
wand, or transfer to a blender. Cool, then store in
screw-top jars.
MAKES 4 CUPS

note: Nectarine, plum or apricot purée can
be substituted for the peach.

tiffin time

(LATE LUNCH)

'One moment bid the horses wait,
Since tiffin is not laid till three'

A BALLADE OF JAKKO HILL RUDYARD KIPLING (1865-1936)

Lacy Chive Pancakes

2 cups (300g/10oz) besan (chickpea) flour
    (plain or wholemeal flour is also suitable)
³/₄ cup (100g/3½oz) coconut milk powder
1 teaspoon salt
1 tablespoon peanut oil
4 large free-range eggs
1½ cups (375ml/12fl oz) cold water
½ cup chopped chives
Ghee for cooking

Combine all ingredients except chives and ghee in a blender or mixing bowl with a pouring spout. Blend or beat until smooth. Stir in chives. Pour mixture into a large plastic squeeze bottle. (Mixture can be refrigerated for several hours or overnight at this stage.)

Heat a griddle iron or heavy-based frying pan over a medium heat. Brush surface with a light coating of ghee. Squirt prepared mixture onto a hot surface to make lacy pancakes (you can make standard solid shapes if you prefer, or if you don't have a squeeze bottle). Cook until top surface begins to look set. Flip and cook other side until golden. Remove from pan and stack while cooking remaining mixture.

Place in a lidded carrying container (or a stacking tiffin container if you have one) and serve at room temperature.

MAKES ABOUT 30 LACY PANCAKES

Spiced Chicken

1.3kg (2lb 10oz) free-range chicken

Paste

5cm (2in) piece green ginger, peeled and
    grated (or 3 tablespoons preserved ginger
    from Ginger and Lime Drinks recipe, p55)

6 green onions, trimmed and roughly chopped

1 tablespoon mild curry powder

2 tablespoons mustard seed oil

½ cup (60g/2oz) coconut milk powder

1 stalk lemon grass, roughly chopped

1 clove garlic

¼ cup (60ml/2fl oz) water

Trim excess fat from body cavity of chicken.

Combine paste ingredients in a blender or food processor and process until smooth. Pour half the mixture into chicken cavity. Tie legs over opening.

Carefully loosen breast and neck skin from chicken flesh without breaking the skin. Push remaining paste under skin, 'massaging' it over chicken flesh as much as possible. Cover and stand at least one hour, or overnight.

Preheat oven to 180°C (350°F/Gas Mark 4). Place chicken on rack positioned over roasting dish. Place in oven and cook for 1 hour. The skin will be a darker brown where the paste is.

Remove from oven. Wrap in foil and then waxed paper. Place in a lidded carrying (or tiffin) container for transportation. Serve at room temperature.

SERVES 4

Apricot Chutney

3kg (6 lb) apricots, stoned
5cm (2in) piece green ginger, peeled and
    grated (or use 3 tablespoons preserved)
1.5kg (3 lb) dark brown sugar
500g (1 lb) palm sugar, roughly chopped
7.5cm (3in) piece cinnamon stick
2 tablespoons sea salt flakes
1 teaspoon ground cloves
2 birds eye chillies (small red) chopped
5 cups (1.25L/2 pints) water
2 medium red (Spanish) onions,
    peeled and chopped
4 cardamom pods, slightly crushed

Combine all ingredients in a large pot. Stir over
high heat until sugar has dissolved. Reduce heat
and simmer, uncovered, for 2-2½ hours, until
mixture is thick and sticky.

Spoon into sterilised screw-top jars and seal.
Store in a cool dark place. Keeps well for up to
12 months.

MAKES ABOUT 3KG

Pressed Rice Cake with Kolonji

1½ cups (300g/10oz) medium grain rice
4 cups (1L/1¾ pints) chicken stock
2 teaspoons dry-roasted kolonji seeds
    (dry roast in a small pan for 2 minutes)

Rinse rice under cold running water until water
runs clear.

Place in a deep saucepan with chicken stock.
Bring to a boil. Cook, partly covered and stirring
occasionally until liquid is absorbed, about
15 minutes. Stir in kolonji seeds. Stand off the
heat, covered, for 10 minutes.

Line a mould with double thickness of clean,
damp muslin. Spoon rice into mould, packing
down firmly. Cover rice with muslin overhang.
Refrigerate several hours or overnight. Carry
in mould or remove muslin-wrapped rice to
another container. Serve at room temperature,
sliced into wedges.

SERVES 4-6

Crisp Fried Onion

4 medium brown onions, peeled
2L (3½ pints) vegetable oil

Using a mandolin or v-cutter, or a very sharp
knife, cut onions into very thin rings.

Heat oil in a deep pot, carefully add onion
and fry in two batches, until dark golden, about
15 minutes each.

Remove with a wire scoop or slotted spoon and
drain on paper towels.

Transfer to a lidded container (or tiffin) for
transportation.

Store at room temperature.

SERVES 4

catching butterflies

(A F T E R N O O N T E A)

'Literature and butterflies are
the two sweetest passions known to man.'

VLADIMIR NABOKOV (1899-1977)

Lemon Buttermilk Tarts

Pastry

1 cup (150g/5oz) plain flour

1 tablespoon pure icing sugar

125g (4oz) unsalted butter

1 free-range egg yolk

1 tablespoon lemon juice

Filling

2 free-range egg yolks

½ cup (110g/3½oz) raw caster sugar

Seeds from ½ vanilla pod (place scraped
    pod in jar of sugar to scent it vanilla)

3 tablespoons plain flour

2 tablespoons unsalted butter,
    melted and cooled

¼ teaspoon baking soda

300ml (10fl oz) cultured buttermilk

1 tablespoon finely grated lemon rind

1 tablespoon lemon juice

Icing sugar, for dusting

For pastry, sift flour and icing sugar into a bowl.
Cut in butter with two knives, and then stir in
combined yolk and lemon juice. Mix until pastry
begins to cling together (if dry add 1 tablespoon
chilled water). Shape into a disc, wrap in plastic and
refrigerate 30 minutes. Roll pastry to line 4 x 10cm
(4in) flan tins. Prick bases and chill 15 minutes (or
cover and freeze, or refrigerate for up to 24 hours).

Preheat oven to 190°C (375°F/Gas Mark 4).
Line pastry cases with baking paper and fill
with baking weights, dried beans or rice. Bake
15 minutes, remove from oven and remove paper
and weights. Return to oven to dry bases, about
5-8 minutes.

Meanwhile, prepare filling.

Whisk yolks until pale and thick. Beat in
combined sugar, vanilla seeds and flour until
smooth, then whisk in butter. Stir baking soda into
buttermilk, stir this mixture into egg mixture, and
then stir in lemon rind and juice.

Reduce oven temperature to 160°C (325°F/
Gas Mark 3).

Pour prepared filling into hot pastry cases and
bake 25-30 minutes, or until filling is set in centre
(test by gently shaking tin—if there is a 'wobble' in
centre of filling, cook tart 5 minutes more).

Remove from oven, place on a wire rack and
cool at room temperature. Refrigerate in tins.
Stack tarts vertically in a plastic container,
separated by waxed paper.

Pack a small shaker of icing sugar and drift icing
sugar over each tart as you serve it.

MAKES 4 TARTS

Surprise Cakes

3 large free-range eggs, separated
110g (3½oz) raw caster sugar
110g (3½oz) dark cooking chocolate, melted
110g (3½oz) coarsely ground walnuts
10 frozen raspberries

Topping
110g (3½oz) dark cooking chocolate, melted
2 tablespoons pure icing sugar, sifted
1 cup (125g/4oz) roasted walnuts,
    finely chopped

Preheat oven to 180°C (350°F/Gas Mark 4).

Beat yolks with sugar until pale and smooth.
Stir in cooled chocolate until thoroughly blended.

Whisk egg whites to form soft peaks, and fold
into chocolate mixture until well incorporated.
Fold in walnuts.

Line 10 x ½ cup (125ml/4fl oz) muffin tins with
paper cases. Spoon mixture into cases to half-fill
each. Place a frozen raspberry in centre and top
with more mixture to cover it.

Cook 15-20 minutes or until firm to touch.
Remove cakes from tin and cool on a wire rack.

For topping, mix chocolate and icing sugar until
smooth. Spread some over the top of each cake,
then press top of cake into walnuts. Leave on wire
rack for 30 minutes, or until topping is set. Pack
cakes into a lidded carrying container and
refrigerate until required.
MAKES 10

Tiny Caramel Toffee Pears

8 firm, ripe 'Golden' pears
    (a tiny variety of pear, with yellow skin)
1 cup (220g/7oz) vanilla caster sugar
¾ cup (190ml/6fl oz) light corn syrup
1 cup (250ml/8fl oz) thickened cream
2 tablespoons unsalted butter
8 wooden ice-block sticks

Make sure pears are at room temperature, and
quite dry. Push a wooden ice-block stick into top
end of each, far enough into pear to be secure.

Combine remaining ingredients in a deep pot,
heat until simmering and stir occasionally until
sugar and butter have dissolved.

Boil 8-10 minutes, or until mixture reaches
120°C (250°F) on a candy thermometer, or toffee
forms a ball when a small drop is put into a glass
of cold water.

Remove from heat and immediately dip pears,
turning them in toffee to achieve an even coating.
Allow any excess to drip off. Place pears on a flat
surface lined with baking paper, until set. You will
need to work quickly or toffee could solidify
before you finish. Pour any surplus toffee onto a
sheet of foil to set.

Place set toffee pears in paper patty cases and
then wrap individually in baking paper for
transportation. Toffee pears are best eaten on the
day they are made.
MAKES 8

Iced Fresh Citrus Drink

Juice a combination of citrus: ruby grapefruit,
lime, lemon and orange, and add sugar to taste.
Pour into a plastic bottle to three-quarters full
and freeze. Use as an ice-block when packing
other food. Make sure you give it enough time to
become sludgy and pourable before you use it.

car travel

from the boot (morning tea)
on the road (lunch)
sticky fingers (afternoon tea)
at twilight (dinner)

~

autumn camping

after a mushroom hunt (brunch)
'campuccino' break (morning coffee)
camp soup (lunch)
fireside feast (dinner)
one pot wonder (dinner)

autumn

from the boot

(MORNING TEA)

'For my part, I travel not to go anywhere, but to go.
I travel for travel's sake. The great affair is to move.'

TRAVELS WITH A DONKEY IN THE CERVENNES ROBERT LOUIS STEVENSON (1850-1894).

Polvorones

125g (4oz) unsalted butter,
    at room temperature
125g (4oz) lard, at room temperature
½ cup (110g/3½oz) caster sugar
Finely grated rind of 1 medium orange
2 large egg yolks
½ cup (125ml/4fl oz) strained fresh
    orange juice
2 cups (300g/10½oz) plain flour
2 cups (300g/10½oz) freshly ground
    almond meal

Preheat oven to 200°C (400°F/Gas Mark 5).

To make these delicious buttery biscuits, beat together butter, lard, caster sugar and orange rind, until pale and fluffy. Add yolks individually, beating well after each addition. Stir in orange juice to combine, then stir in combined flour and almond meal until mixture clings together.

Turn mixture out onto a sheet of baking paper on the work surface. Shape it into a rectangle. Place another sheet of baking paper on top, press gently with your hands until dough is 2cm (¾in) thick. Using a floured 3cm (1¼in) round biscuit cutter, cut polvorones and place on a baking tray. Re-roll scraps, and cut until all dough is used.

Bake for 15 minutes. Cool on tray. Pack into an airtight container when cold.

MAKES 24

note: Rolling sticky dough or marzipan between sheets of baking paper makes handling much easier, with less mess.

Olive Oil and Caraway Seed Loaf with Quark

2 cups (300g/10½oz) wholemeal plain flour
2 teaspoons baking powder
1 tablespoon raw sugar
1 tablespoon caraway seeds
Finely grated rind of 1 medium lemon
1 cup (250ml/8fl oz) olive oil
½ cup (125ml/4fl oz) milk
3 eggs, separated
Quark, to serve

Preheat oven to 180°C (350°F/Gas Mark 4).
 Lightly spray a 6-cup (1.5L/3 pint) loaf tin
with oil. Line base with baking paper.
 Combine flour, baking powder, sugar, caraway
seeds and lemon rind in a bowl.
 Whisk together oil, milk and egg yolks. Stir
in flour mixture until thoroughly combined.
 Whisk egg whites until soft peaks form. Fold
into loaf mixture until smooth. Spoon into
prepared loaf tin, bake in centre of oven for
30 minutes, or until a metal skewer inserted
into cake comes out clean. Cool for 5 minutes
in tin, before turning out onto a wire rack.
SERVES 8

note: Quark is a fresh, soft white cheese,
similar to but softer than cream cheese.
It has a slightly sour taste, and is available
from supermarkets and delicatessens.

Little Coconut Lime Cakes

125g (4oz) unsalted butter,
    at room temperature
1 cup (220g/7½oz) caster sugar
Finely grated rind of 2 limes
3 large eggs, at room temperature
2 cups (170g/6oz) desiccated coconut
1 cup (150g/5oz) unbleached self-raising flour

Icing
1 cup (160g/5½oz) pure icing sugar, sifted
60g (2oz) butter, at room temperature
1-2 tablespoons lime juice
Finely julienned rind of 1 lime, for decoration

Preheat oven to 180°C (350°F/Gas Mark 4).

Line 2½ small patty trays (30 cups) with paper cases. Lightly spray inside each one with oil.

Beat butter, sugar and rind until pale and fluffy. Add eggs individually, beating well after each addition. Fold in combined coconut and flour, until thoroughly mixed.

Spoon 1 tablespoon of the cake mixture into each patty case, then bake for 15 minutes. Cool before icing.

To make icing, combine icing sugar and butter and mix to a smooth paste. Slowly mix in lime juice to desired consistency. Place a teaspoonful on each cake. Decorate with julienned rind of lime. Transport cakes in the patty baking tins, wrapped in a cloth or plastic.

MAKES 30

on the road

'Does the road wind uphill all the way?
Yes, to the very end.
Will the day's journey take the whole long day?
From morn to night, my friend.'

UP-HILL CHRISTINA GEORGINA ROSSETTI (1830-1894).

Spanish Omelette

1½ cups (375ml/12fl oz) olive oil
1kg (2 lb) potatoes (suitable for boiling),
    peeled and cut into 1cm (½in) dice
3 medium Spanish (red) onions,
    chopped to give 2½ cups
10 large free-range eggs
12 large caperberries, stalks removed
    and berries halved
1 tablespoon sea salt
½ teaspoon freshly ground black pepper

Heat oil in a 30cm (12in) diameter, heavy-based
(non-stick if available) deep frying or ovenproof
pan, until hot, but not smoking.

Combine potato and onion and carefully add to
the pan and cook over a medium-low heat for
35 minutes, stirring occasionally, or until potatoes
are very tender.

Transfer mixture to a colander positioned over a
bowl, and drain. Reserve oil. Wash frying pan.

Whisk eggs with 1 tablespoon of the drained oil.
Add slightly cooled potato and onion mixture and
caperberries. Season with salt and freshly ground
black pepper.

Heat frying pan and add another tablespoon of
the drained oil. Pour in egg mixture and cook over
a medium-low heat for 8-10 minutes, shaking pan
occasionally to prevent base from sticking.

If you have an ovenproof pan, heat the grill and
cook the top of the omelette until golden and
puffed, and the centre of the omelette is set. If
using a standard frying pan cover omelette with a
large plate and stand (off the heat) for 10 minutes,
then invert omelette onto plate. If sticking, use
a long metal spatula to free the base. Slide
omelette, base up, back into pan and cook gently
for a further 5-8 minutes, or until set.

Transport omelette in pan, or transfer to a
large plate. Serve, sliced into wedges, at room
temperature. The omelette keeps well for 2 days
if refrigerated.
SERVES 6-8

note: Pitted black olives could be added to
this mixture, or substituted for the
caperberries.

Paprika Tomatoes

8 ripe, firm Roma tomatoes
4 teaspoons paprika
4 teaspoons sea salt
4 teaspoons olive oil

Cut each tomato in half around the equator. Using a sharp knife, score a grid pattern in the cut surface. Sprinkle ½ teaspoon each of the paprika, salt and oil onto each tomato, then rub the cut surfaces of two halves together to blend in the mixture. Repeat with all tomatoes. Place tomatoes in a storage container for transportation and seal. Serve at room temperature.
SERVES 8

note: These tomatoes will keep for 1 week, if refrigerated. They produce their own 'dressing', a combination of the oil and tomato juice. They are delicious chopped and stirred through freshly cooked pasta with canned tuna chunks, black olives, chopped caperberries or capers, chopped Italian (flat-leaf) parsley and shaved Parmesan.

Charred Eggplant and Mint Salad

2 large eggplants (aubergines), about 1kg (2 lb)
1 tablespoon aniseed
½ cup (125ml/4fl oz) mustard seed oil
1 cup torn mint leaves

Wash eggplant and cut into 2.5cm (1in) dice. Combine with aniseed.

Heat a ribbed iron grill pan until smoking (or a barbecue for a delicious smoky flavour). Toss batches of eggplant in a little mustard seed oil and char-grill (avoid leaving eggplant in oil for too long as it will absorb too much of it). The cooked eggplant will be charred but retain its shape.

Layer hot eggplant with mint leaves, finishing with the leaves on top, in a storage container for transportation. Seal container when eggplant is cold. Serve at room temperature.
SERVES 6-8

note: This salad will keep well for 1 week if refrigerated. Taste your mustard seed oil for its flavour strength—some brands are more potent than others. Dilute the oil with canola oil if necessary. The prepared eggplant and mint can be cooked with diced barbecue chicken in a frittata, stirred through cooked pasta with green peas and shaved Parmesan, used as a filling ingredient in home-made hamburgers, or stirred through a risotto towards the end of cooking.

Olive Bread Rolls

2 sachets (14g–16g/½oz) active dried yeast
1½ cups (375ml/12fl oz) lukewarm milk
1 tablespoon brown sugar
4 cups (600g/1¼lb) unbleached white
    bread flour
½ teaspoon salt
1 teaspoon freshly ground black pepper
1 egg, whisked
¼ cup (60ml/2fl oz) garlic oil (see recipe p118,
    include garlic cloves for a stronger flavour)
¾–1 cup black olives, pitted and sliced
Extra flour for dusting moulds

Combine yeast with milk and sugar in a small
bowl. Stand in a draft-free place for 10 minutes,
or until mixture is frothy.

Combine flour, salt and pepper in a large mixing
bowl. Add yeast mixture, egg and garlic oil (and
cloves, if using) in one lot, then stir until well
incorporated. Knead dough for 10 minutes on a
floured surface, or use an electric mixer fitted
with a dough hook, on low speed for 10 minutes.

Add olives and knead to incorporate without
mashing them.

Turn dough into a lightly floured ceramic or
glass bowl. Cover with a clean tea towel (kitchen
cloth) and stand in a warm, draft-free position for
one hour, or until dough is doubled in bulk. Punch
down, turn onto a floured surface and knead into
a log. Cut into 15 equal parts. Lightly spray 15
large muffin trays or 15 x ¾ cup (175ml/6fl oz)
individual moulds with oil. Sprinkle flour through
a sieve over trays or moulds. Tap out excess flour.
Place individual moulds on a baking tray.

Preheat oven to 190˚C (375˚F/Gas Mark 4).

Knead each piece of dough into a ball and place
in a mould. Cover with a cloth and stand again for
30 minutes or until well risen. Brush tops lightly
with cold water.

Bake in preheated oven for 15 minutes, until
golden and crisp. Cool in tins for 5 minutes, then
turn out onto a wire rack. Wrap in a clean cloth
for transportation, with a container of butter.
MAKES 15

note: Use a cherry pipper to pit olives, or if
you don't have one, just slice the flesh away
from the stone. Sliced stuffed green olives,
or marinated olives, can also be used, for a
more complex flavour.

Nectarine Marzipan Tarts

1 sheet ready-rolled frozen puff pastry, thawed
60g (2oz) marzipan, at room temperature
8 baked nectarine halves (see note)
30g (1oz) butter, at room temperature
Icing sugar, to serve

Preheat oven to 200°C (400°F/Gas Mark 5).

Lightly spray 8 x ⅓ cup (80ml/2½fl oz) muffin tins with oil. Cut 8 rounds from the pastry, the same diameter as the top of tins. Place in tins.

Roll marzipan between two sheets of baking paper, until very thin. Cut 8 x 2.5cm (1in) rounds and place one in each pastry case. Place a nectarine half, cut side up, in each case and smear tops with a little butter.

Bake 12-15 minutes, or until pastry is puffed and golden. When cool, store in an airtight container for transportation. The tarts will keep for 1-2 days.

Serve at room temperature dusted lightly with icing sugar.

MAKES 8

note: Baked nectarine halves are virtually oven-dried nectarines. The flavour is intensified and the texture firm. To bake, halve firm, ripe nectarines. Remove stone (a serrated grapefruit spoon is good for this) and place fruit, cut-side-up in a single layer on a non-stick oven tray (or conventional tray lined with baking paper). Bake at 150°C (300°F/Gas Mark 2) for 2–3 hours. Cool on tray, then store in an airtight container in the refrigerator. They will keep for several weeks. Alternatively, add port to the container and refrigerate.

Use baked nectarines as a simple dessert, with clotted cream, custard or ice-cream; or bake in a flan with a whisked egg, cream and sugar filling; or in a breakfast fruit compote; or straight from the fridge at midnight!

Large, late season plums and whole firm figs are also delicious baked this way and served warm with Tamarillo Mascarpone Ice-cream (see recipe p103).

Lime Refresher

12 limes
1 cup (220g/7oz) raw sugar
½ teaspoon salt

Wash limes. Roll each lime on a work surface, pressing down as you do, to break the membranes (the fruit gives off more juice this way). Cut limes in half around the equator, squeeze juice through a sieve, into a jug. Place squeezed halves in a large bowl with sugar and salt. Cover halves with 6 cups (1.5L/48fl oz) boiling water, stir to dissolve sugar and stand for 10 minutes only (any longer and the drink will become bitter).

Strain this liquid into the juice. Refrigerate in a screw- or clip-top bottle.

Serve on lots of ice and garnish with mint sprigs, or mix with tonic, ginger ale or soda and ice as a long drink.

MAKES 2L/3½ pints

sticky fingers

(A F T E R N O O N   T E A)

'Take some more tea,' the March Hare said to Alice, very earnestly.
'I've had nothing yet,' Alice replied in an offended tone,
'so I can't take more.'

ALICE'S ADVENTURES IN WONDERLAND LEWIS CARROLL (1832-1898)

Fig Tart

Base

1½ cups (200g/6½oz) walnut pieces,
    finely ground
1 cup (150g/5oz) plain flour (gluten-free flour
    is suitable)
¼ cup (75g/2½oz) brown sugar,
    firmly packed
60g (2oz) butter, melted and cooled
1 egg, separated
1 tablespoon lemon juice

Filling

26 small figs, fresh or caramelised (see note)
4 eggs, plus 1 egg white, from base ingredients
60g (2oz) butter, melted and cooled
¾ cup (190ml/6fl oz) dark corn syrup (or
    reserved fig syrup, if using caramelised figs)

Place rack in centre of oven and preheat oven to
190°C (375°F/Gas Mark 4).

Lightly spray a 23cm (9in) diameter deep flan
tin with oil.

For base, combine walnut, flour and brown
sugar in a bowl. Whisk together butter, egg
yolk and lemon juice, then stir into dry
ingredients. Press into base of flan tin and bake
for 15 minutes.

Meanwhile, whisk together eggs, egg white,
butter and corn or fig syrup. Place tart tin on a
pizza or baking tray in case filling leaks. Place
figs on hot tart base, pour filling mixture carefully
around them to almost reach top of tin. Bake for
45 minutes, until filling is set in centre.

Cool tart in tin, then loosen base by sliding
a metal spatula between it and edge of tin.
Transport tart in tin, remove ring and serve from
metal base.

The tart is best if eaten within 48 hours, but will
keep for up to 1 week, refrigerated.

SERVES 8-10

note: For a more intense, sticky flavour,
cook figs in a single layer in a covered,
large deep pan. For 26 small figs, add
½ cup (100g/3½oz) brown sugar and ¼ cup
(60ml/2fl oz) water, and cook over medium
heat, shaking pan occasionally. Remove lid,
reduce heat to low and cook a further
20 minutes. Cool. Refrigerate figs and syrup
in an airtight container for up to 10 days.
Caramelised figs are also delicious used as
a dessert with cream or ice-cream, in
individual tarts with commercial puff pastry
and a filling of cream whisked with egg and
brown sugar.

Pistachio Rose Biscuits

250g (8oz) unsalted butter, at room
    temperature
⅓ cup (150g/5oz) caster sugar
1 teaspoon rosewater
100g (3½oz) peeled and shelled fresh
    pistachios, coarsely ground (see note)
2 cups (300g/10½oz) unbleached plain flour

Preheat oven to 160°C (325°F/Gas Mark 3).
    Beat butter with sugar until pale and fluffy. Beat
in rosewater. Stir in nuts and flour, until mixture
clings together.
    Place a sheet of baking paper on a work surface,
turn dough onto it and cover with another sheet
of paper. Press dough down to about 1cm (½in)
thick. Cut shapes with a floured 5cm (2in) biscuit
cutter. Re-roll scraps and repeat until all dough is
used. Place biscuits on a baking tray, score tops
with the back of a knife and bake 20 minutes,
until pale golden. Cool on tray for 5 minutes, then
transfer to a wire rack to cool completely. Store in
an airtight container for transportation.
MAKES ABOUT 30

note: Fresh pistachios have a short season,
but are well worth trying. The outer husk
slips off easily, to reveal the familiar shell.
Inside is the raw nut (kernel) which can be
used as is, in baking or eaten uncooked.
Dried pistachio kernels can be substituted
in this recipe—the biscuit texture will be
slightly crunchier.
    To roast fresh pistachios, peel the outer
husk and place nuts in their shells in a single
layer on an oven tray. Toss with pistachio or
another nut oil or olive oil, to coat lightly.
Sprinkle with fine salt and roast at 190°C
(375°F/Gas Mark 4) for 20 minutes, stirring
occasionally, until crisp. When cold, store
in an airtight container.
    The nuts can also be cooked over a
campfire or barbecue for a slightly rustic,
smokier flavour.

Little Sugar Sponges

½ cup (75g/2½oz) plain flour
1¼ cups (275g/8½oz) caster sugar
Finely grated rind of 1 lemon
5 eggs, at room temperature, separated
Caster sugar, extra

Line 12 x ½ cup (125ml/4fl oz) muffin tins
with paper cases.
    Preheat oven to 180°C (350°F/Gas Mark 4).
Sift flour into the bowl of an electric mixer.
Add 1 cup (220g/7oz) of the caster sugar, lemon
rind and the egg yolks. Whisk until thick and

pale—about 3–5 minutes. (The mixture will seem dry at first, but will soon break down when whisked.)

Wash whisks, then beat egg whites until stiff. Add remaining sugar to whites, beating until mixture is smooth and glossy. Stir about one-third of this mixture into yolk mixture, then carefully fold in remainder.

Spoon into cases, to almost fill each one. Sprinkle tops with extra caster sugar and bake for 15 minutes. Best eaten the same day.

MAKES 12

Tamarillo Sauce

6 tamarillos
Raw sugar to taste

Score an 'X' on the base of each tamarillo. Place in a deep saucepan, add 1 cup (250ml/ 8fl oz) water, cover pan and bring to a simmer. Cook 20 minutes over a low heat until fruit is beginning to peel and water is a deep pink colour.

Remove pan from heat; pick up each tamarillo by its stem and using a small, sharp knife, cut across top of tamarillo just under the stem. The fruit should fall away and the stem and skin remain in one piece. Discard these. Blend fruit and liquid in pan, using a food processing wand, or transfer to a blender. Strain purée through a coarse sieve. Discard seeds. Taste and stir sugar (or honey) into warm sauce if desired.

Pour into a sealable jug or bottle for transportation. The sauce keeps well for up to 2 weeks, if refrigerated.

MAKES 2 CUPS (500ml/16fl oz)

note: Use the sauce for tamarillo ice-cream (recipe follows) or sorbet; freeze sauce for use out of season; use it to accompany poached autumn fruits, such as nectarines, pears or plums.

Tamarillo Mascarpone Ice-cream

2 large egg yolks
½ cup (110g/3½oz) caster sugar
½ cup (125ml/4fl oz) full-cream milk
375g (12oz) fresh mascarpone
1½ cups (375ml/12fl oz) tamarillo sauce
(see recipe opposite)

Whisk yolks and sugar until pale and thick. Gradually whisk in milk, then mascarpone. Whisk in tamarillo sauce.

Pour into an ice-cream maker and churn according to manufacturer's instructions. Spoon into a container, cover and freeze until required. Alternatively, pour into a shallow freezer container, freeze until semi-set (about 30 minutes), whisk with a fork to break up ice particles and re-freeze. Repeat this process three times before finally freezing. Remove ice-cream from freezer to refrigerator at least 30 minutes before serving to soften.

MAKES 4 CUPS (1L/1¾ pints)

at twilight

(DINNER)

'So, we'll go no more a-roving
So late into the night,
Though the heart be still as loving,
And the moon still be as bright.'

SO WE'LL GO NO MORE A-ROVING LORD BYRON (1788-1824)

Individual Onion and Parmesan Tarts

Pastry
2½ cups (375g/12oz) plain flour
⅓ cup (50g/1½oz) finely grated Parmesan
90g (3oz) butter
½ cup (125ml/4fl oz) cold water

Filling
¼ cup (60ml/2fl oz) olive oil
1 tablespoon butter
12 medium brown onions, very finely sliced
½ whole nutmeg, freshly grated
Leaves from 4 sprigs fresh thyme
4 large eggs
250g (8oz) sour cream
⅓ cup (50g/1½oz) finely grated Parmesan

For pastry, combine flour and Parmesan in a large bowl. Rub in butter until mixture resembles fine breadcrumbs. Stir in cold water to form a firm dough. Knead into a disc, wrap in plastic and refrigerate for about 20 minutes.

Preheat oven to 190°C (375°F/Gas Mark 4).

Roll pastry until thin on a lightly floured surface and cut to fit 8 x 10cm (4in) individual tart tins. Re-roll scraps to use all pastry. Line tins with baking paper and fill with baking weights, dried beans or rice. Cook 15 minutes, remove paper and weights. Return to oven for 2 minutes, to dry base.

For filling, heat oil and butter in a heavy-based frying pan, over medium heat. Add onion, nutmeg and thyme, stir to coat with oil. Cover pan and cook over low heat for 45 minutes, stirring occasionally. The onion will become golden and slightly caramelised. Remove from heat to cool slightly. Whisk together eggs, cream, and Parmesan. Stir in onion, then spoon into prepared pastry bases. Bake in oven for 30 minutes, or until centre of filling is set. Serve warm or at room temperature.

SERVES 8

note: This recipe can be made as one large tart in a 23cm (9in) flan tin. Cook with filling 40–45 minutes, or until centre is set. The onion can be cooked 1–2 days before required, and refrigerated.

The best result will be obtained if the filling is ready and spooned into the hot pastry shells after they have been baked blind. This helps the base remain crisp.

The onion can also be used as an omelette filling, or hot with cooked meat. The best finely sliced onion is obtained by using a v-cutter (or mandolin cutter), a tool available from most kitchen shops. Not only is the onion very thin, but the slicing is achieved very quickly, which to some degree eliminates 'onion tears'.

The most efficient way of trimming raw pastry from a tart tin, is to lay rolled pastry over the tin, gently pressing in to base and sides, leaving a small overhang. Press a rolling pin over the edges of the tin to cleanly cut the edge of the pastry.

Roast Lemon Chicken

2 x 1.3kg (2 lb) free-range chickens
2 teaspoons sea salt
1 teaspoon ground coriander
½ teaspoon saffron threads
2 tablespoons mustard seed oil
½ cup (125ml/4fl oz) cold water

Stuffing
2 thin-skinned lemons, chopped,
    seeds removed
1 medium onion, peeled and quartered
1 clove garlic, peeled
125g (4½oz) Turkish bread, cut into
    2cm (¾in) cubes
1 teaspoon ground coriander
1 tablespoon mustard seed oil

To make stuffing, combine ingredients in a blender or food processor and work to a coarse paste.

Preheat oven to 180°C (350°F/Gas Mark 4).

Rinse chicken under cold running water, remove giblets and trim excess skin from neck and fat from inside cavity. Pat dry, then spoon the stuffing mixture into each chicken. Pull skin flap over opening, tie feet together with kitchen string to secure. (If you like, some stuffing can be pushed through the neck opening and under the breast skin.) Tuck neck skin flaps under chickens, then place birds on a rack in a roasting dish.

Combine sea salt, ground coriander and saffron in a mortar and grind, slowly adding 2 tablespoons mustard seed oil. Brush mixture over chickens. Pour a little water into roasting dish, then place chickens in oven and roast 1-1¼ hours. Wrap in foil for transportation. Serve at room temperature.
SERVES 8

Chickpea and Rice Terrine

1½ cups (300g/10oz) medium grain rice
3 cups (750ml/24fl oz) chicken stock
2 x 300g (10oz) cans chickpeas, drained
1 tablespoon green peppercorns
½ cup (100g/3½oz) sun-dried tomatoes, diced
    and 1 tablespoon of their oil
½ cup (80g/2½ oz) stoned kalamata olives

Combine rice and stock in a deep saucepan.
Bring to a boil, stir. Reduce heat, partly cover
and simmer for 10 minutes, stirring occasionally.
Preheat oven to 180°C (350°F/Gas Mark 4).
Combine rice with remaining ingredients, then
pack into an oiled 6-cup (1.5L/48fl oz) terrine or
loaf tin. Cover closely with foil.

  Place in a baking dish, pour in water until 1cm
(½in) up side of terrine. Bake 20-30 minutes, cool
slightly then turn out onto a serving plate, or
once released, return to tin for transportation.
SERVES 8

Quince in Jelly with Mascarpone

4 quince, washed to remove down, then cut
    into quarters
1 lemon, thickly sliced
1 cup (220g/7½ oz) raw sugar
15g (½oz) gelatine sheets
Mascarpone, to serve

Heat oven to 150°C (300°F/Gas Mark 2).

  Place quince, lemon and sugar in a deep, heavy-
based ovenproof pan or saucepan. Cover quince
with about 4 cups (1L/32fl oz) water. Heat until
simmering. Cover pot and transfer to oven for
3-4 hours, until quince are tender and a deep
pink colour (or cook over low heat on burner or
element—I prefer the oven as there is minimal risk
of quince boiling dry). Remove cooked quince
from liquid and cool until easy to handle. Peel and
remove cores. Cut into 1cm (½in) dice.

  Soak gelatine sheets in cold water for about
2 minutes. Squeeze out excess water and combine
gelatine with 3 cups (750ml/24fl oz) of the
strained quince cooking liquid. Stir over a low
heat until gelatine has dissolved. Divide diced
quince between 8 x ½ cup (125ml/4fl oz) glasses.
Pour liquid into each to fill to brim, releasing any
air pockets with a skewer. Place on a tray and
refrigerate until set (1-2 hours). Serve in individual
glasses with mascarpone passed separately.
SERVES 8

note: If you prefer, make up one large
jelly and either unmould it or serve straight
from the container. Once set, the jellies will
remain firm for several hours at room
temperature, in the glasses. To transport
individual jellies, place glasses on a tray or
in a shallow container, each wrapped with
a napkin to provide packing.

  Quince are best when a deep yellow colour
with no visible blemishes. They can be
cooked overnight at 100-120°C (250°F/
Gas Mark 1). Cooking with the skin on makes
peeling very easy (a bit like peeling tomatoes
or tamarillos), eliminates waste and gives a
superior appearance. Cooked quince keep
well, for up to one week, refrigerated in their
juice. Drained, the cooked quince freezes
well, and is suitable for use in cakes, tarts and
purées. The juice can be boiled with extra
sugar to make a thick syrup.

car travel

autumn

after a mushroom hunt

(B R U N C H)

'Have ever you seen on a hillside
The mushroom white and small,
Thrusting her head through the grass,
And the dewdrops over all?'

THE MUSHROOM DAME MARY GILMORE (1835-1962)

Pumpkin Pancakes

2 cups (300g/9½oz) self-raising flour
½ teaspoon ground cumin
Salt and ground white pepper to taste
4 eggs
1 x 420g (13½oz) can condensed creamy
    pumpkin soup
Olive oil and butter, for cooking

Combine flour, cumin, salt and freshly ground
white pepper to taste, in a mixing container.
  Beat eggs and pumpkin soup into flour, adding
enough cold water to give a thick pouring batter.
  Heat a heavy frying pan, melt a little butter and
oil. Make pancakes to desired size, cook on one
side until bubbles appear on the surface. Before
bubbles pop, flip pancake and cook underside
until golden. Serve hot and buttered.
SERVES 6

note: Take dry ingredients, pre-mixed,
in a lidded container large enough to hold
remaining pancake ingredients. Simply add
the eggs, pumpkin and water and mix.
  The whole eggs can be safely carried in the
container of dry ingredients.

Wild Mushrooms with Sausage and Farm Eggs

6 saucisson Lyonnaise (or other spicy sausage)
30g (1oz) butter
2 tablespoons olive oil or mustard seed oil
1 tablespoon caraway seeds
6 cèpe or pine mushrooms, wiped and sliced
6-12 free-range eggs

Heat a frying pan over moderate flame. Add sausages and cook, turning frequently, until crisp. Remove from pan and place on a tin plate (or on double thickness aluminium foil). Cover with another plate and position at the edge of fire to keep warm. (If using tin plates to eat from, take the chill off them by stacking, upturned, on top of the sausages.)

Heat butter and oil in frying pan, add caraway seeds and cook 1 minute, then add mushrooms. Cook over hottest part of fire, stirring frequently, until soft. Remove from pan and keep warm in same manner as sausages.

Break eggs into frying pan and cook to desired firmness (although runny eggs make this meal more luscious).

Place a pumpkin pancake (see recipe p108) and sausage on each plate. Top pancake with egg and then mushroom. Eat immediately.

SERVES 6

Late Plum and Honey Puddings

6 slices sweet brioche (or white bread),
    buttered on both sides
6 Autumn Giant or other late-harvest plums
6 tablespoons honey (orange-blossom, clover,
    or your preference)
Yoghurt, quark or ricotta, to serve

Cut double thickness squares of aluminium foil to generously wrap plums.

In centre of each square, place a slice of brioche and a plum on this. Bring edges of foil up around plum, then spoon over a tablespoon of honey. Close foil over plum like a money pouch, and twist ends to secure.

Scrape a pile of embers to one edge of the fire, bury the parcels and cook for 30-40 minutes. Keep warm. To serve, open parcels carefully, and tip contents into bowls. Top with yoghurt, quark or ricotta.

SERVES 6

note: Prepare and semi-wrap puddings at home. Pack into a lidded plastic container with the honey in a small jar. Finish wrapping at campsite.

'campuccino' break

(MORNING COFFEE)

'When I was young, we always had mornings like this.'

TOAD OF TOAD HALL A.A. MILNE (1882-1956)

Whisky, Walnut and Fig Loaf

25 dried white Greek figs
1 cup (250ml/8fl oz) whisky
½ cup (125ml/4fl oz) walnut oil
   (or other nut oil)
1 cup (200g/6½oz) brown sugar
3 eggs, at room temperature
1 cup (125g/4oz) walnut pieces, crushed
3 cups (450g/14½oz) self-raising flour

Slice figs in half through the equator. Soak halves in whisky for at least three hours, or as long as possible. Drain, reserving any liquid.

Arrange some of the halves cut-side down in one layer to cover the bases of 2 x 6-cup (1.5L/48fl oz) bread tins (18 x 10 x 10cm/7 x 4 x 4in). Chop remaining figs and reserve.

Preheat oven to 180°C (350°F/Gas Mark 4).

Beat walnut oil and sugar to thoroughly combine. Beat in eggs, and then reserved fig liquid, until mixture is thick and pale. Stir in nuts and chopped fig. Sift in flour and mix thoroughly. Spoon into tins on top of sliced figs. Smooth tops.

Bake 35–40 minutes, or until a metal skewer inserted into centre comes out clean. Cool in tins for five minutes, then turn out onto a wire rack to cool completely. Wrap in foil and transport in a sealed container. Loaf keeps well for up to one week.

MAKES 2 LOAVES

Warm Apple Damper

4 cups (600g/1 lb) self-raising flour
1 teaspoon salt
¼ cup (60g/2oz) caster sugar
½ cup (75g/2½oz) full-cream milk powder
1 teaspoon ground cinnamon
¼ teaspoon ground cloves
375ml (12fl oz) jar apple sauce
Apple jelly and butter, to serve

Heat camp or 'Dutch' oven amongst hot coals.
Alternatively, cook in a standard oven at 200°C
(400°F/Gas Mark 5) for 15-20 minutes.

Combine dry ingredients in a mixing container.
Stir in apple sauce and enough water (about ½
cup/125ml/4fl oz) to give a soft, but not sticky,
dough. Pat into a round shape, almost the
diameter of the camp oven. Sprinkle flour over
the inside base of the hot oven. Place dough
inside and then score the top into 8-10 wedges.
Place lid on oven, cover with a shovelful of coals
and cook 30-35 minutes.

Carefully remove lid (brush off coals) and check
if damper is golden and well risen. Return to fire if
necessary. Serve hot, pulled apart, with lashings
of butter and apple jelly (or golden syrup).
SERVES 8-10

note: Chopped walnuts could be added to
dry ingredients, which can be packed and
transported in a lidded container, ready for
the addition of wet ingredients.

Apple Jelly

2kg (4 lb) Golden Delicious or Granny Smith apples
Caster sugar

Quarter apples and place in a large pot with
5 cups (1.25L/2 pints) water. Bring to a simmer and
cook, stirring occasionally, until soft and pulpy.

Place a jelly bag in a large bowl; ladle the apples
and liquid into it. Hang the bag over the bowl,
preferably overnight. Do not squeeze the bag, or
the jelly will cloud.

Measure the juice (discard pulp) and return it to
the cleaned pot. For every 600ml (1 pint) liquid,
add 450g (1 lb) caster sugar.

Heat gently, stirring occasionally, until sugar has
dissolved. Increase heat, boil without stirring
(about 40 minutes). Adjust heat if necessary to
prevent liquid boiling over during cooking
time. Jelly has reached setting point when a
teaspoonful placed on a cold saucer forms a skin,
and remains divided when you have run your
finger through its centre. Skim surface. Pour into
warm sterilised jars, cool, then seal. Store in a
cool place. Keeps for several months.
MAKES ABOUT 6 CUPS (1.5L/48fl oz)

note: When making apple jelly, use 300ml
(½ pint) water for each 500g (1 lb) raw apple.

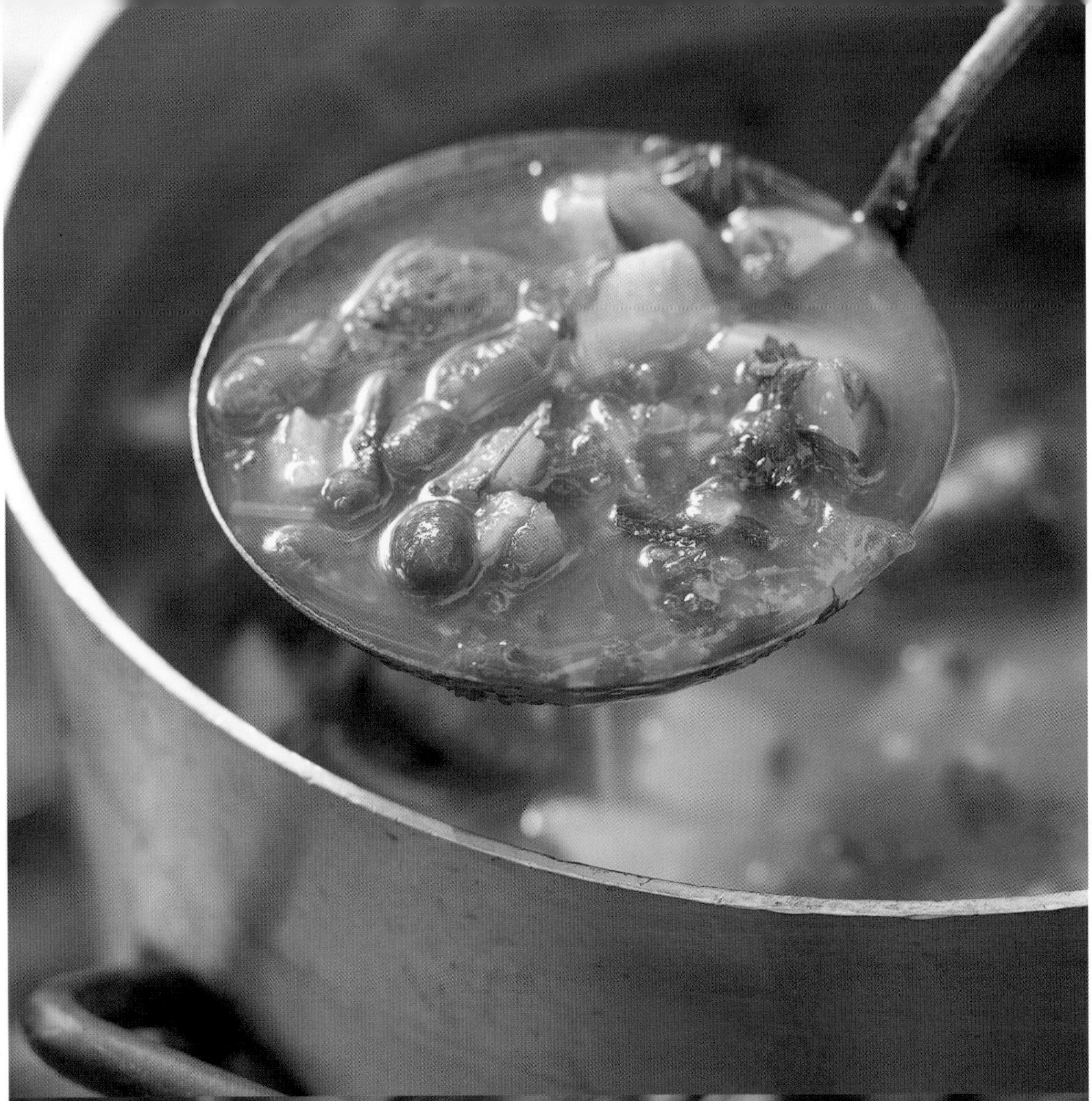

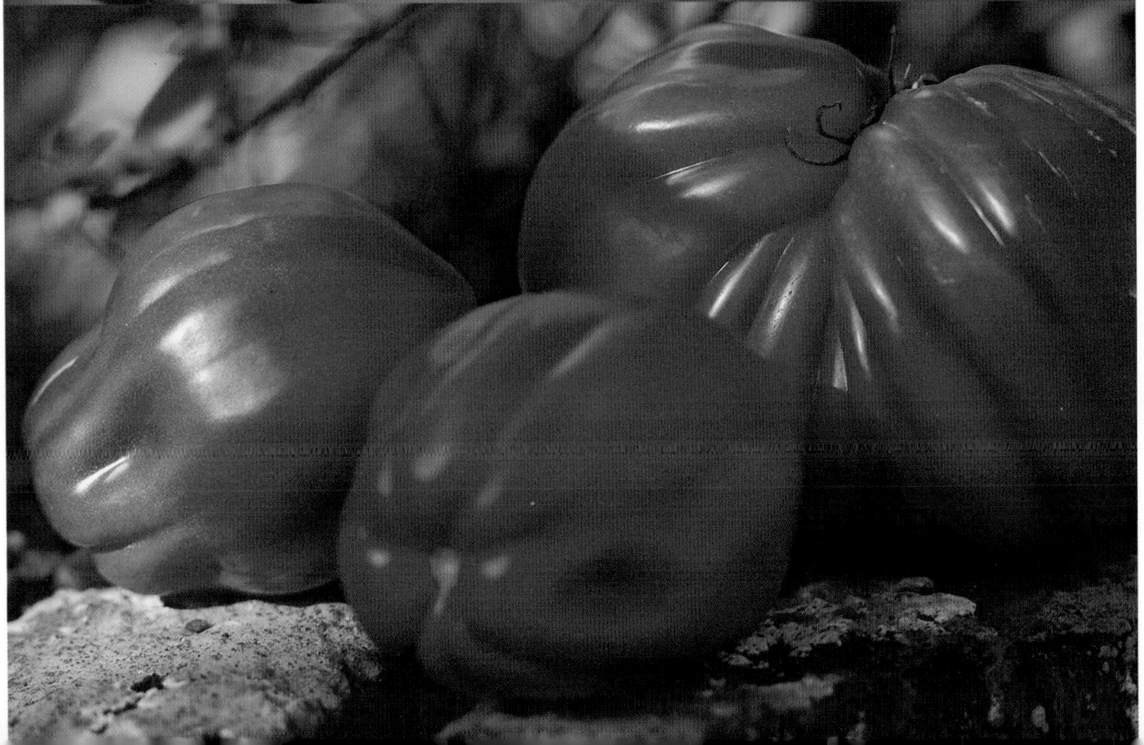

camp soup

'Billy, in one of his nice new sashes,
Fell in the fire and was burnt to ashes;
Now, although the room grows chilly,
I haven't the heart to poke poor Billy.'

'TENDER-HEARTEDNESS' FROM *RUTHLESS RHYMES*
FOR HEARTLESS HOMES HARRY GRAHAM (1874-1936)

Sausage and Borlotti Camp Soup

500g (1 lb) fresh chorizo
300g (9½oz) dried cacciatore or salami sausage
2 large Spanish (red) onions, chopped
1 medium head fennel, diced
1 medium head celeriac, peeled and diced
8 Jerusalem artichokes, peeled and diced
500g (1 lb) fresh borlotti beans (or canned)
6 fresh oxheart tomatoes (beefsteak tomatoes),
    diced (or 2 x 410g/13oz can tomatoes)
2 cups chopped Italian (flat-leaf) parsley

Cut chorizo into thick slices. Remove papery skin from cacciatore and slice sausage, then cut each slice into quarters.

Position a large pot over the fire, add sausage and stir to soften, about 5 minutes. Add onion, fennel, celeriac, Jerusalem artichokes and stir to combine. Cover pot and cook vegetables, stirring occasionally, for about 15 minutes.

Add beans (if using canned, add liquid also) and tomatoes.

Add enough water to cover. Bring to a simmer and cook, partly covered, for 30 minutes. Stir occasionally until vegetables are tender and soup well flavoured.

Just before serving, stir in parsley.

Eat with crusty bread or Dill and Parmesan scones (see recipe p116) made in camp oven.

SERVES 8-10

Ginger Crisps

125g (4oz) butter, at room temperature
1 cup (200g/6½oz) dark brown sugar
2 tablespoons Golden Syrup
1 tablespoon fresh ginger juice (see note)
60g (2oz) glacé ginger, finely chopped
1 cup (150g/5oz) plain flour

Preheat oven to 190°C (375°F/Gas Mark 4).

Spray with oil or lightly butter, 2-3 large biscuit trays (or use non-stick trays).

Beat together butter and sugar until pale and fluffy. Stir in Golden Syrup, ginger juice, glacé ginger and finally flour. Roll scant teaspoonfuls of the mixture into balls. Place, well spaced, onto trays then flatten with the tines of a fork (dip fork into flour to prevent sticking).

Bake 8-10 minutes, until spread and cooked in the centre. Cool on trays for 2 minutes, remove and cool completely on a wire rack. Store in an airtight container. (This quantity will keep crisper if divided amongst small snap-lock plastic bags, then stored in one larger container.)

MAKES 45

note: To make 1 tablespoon ginger juice, grate 60g (2oz) unpeeled fresh ginger, or grind it in an electric nut grinder. Place pulp in centre of a 15cm (6in) square of muslin, bring edges together and twist to form a pouch. As you twist tightly, the juice will drip out.

Dill and Parmesan Scones

3 cups (450g/14½oz) self-raising flour
1 teaspoon salt
100g (3½oz) grated Parmesan
100g (3½oz) butter
2 teaspoons dried dill
¼ cup (60ml/2fl oz) full-cream milk powder
Flour, extra

Heat camp oven in hot coals. Alternatively, cook in a standard oven at 200°C (400°F/Gas Mark 5) for 15-20 minutes.

Combine flour, salt and Parmesan in a mixing container. Add butter and rub in until mixture resembles fine breadcrumbs. Stir in dill and milk powder. (The mixture can be made to this point, covered and transported and stored until required.)

To finish preparation, add 1¼ cups (310ml/10fl oz) water, mix to a soft dough and shape into scone size balls.

Sprinkle base of camp oven with flour. Position scones fairly close together, working from the centre out. Replace oven lid, cover with a shovelful of hot coals and cook 15-20 minutes. Check after 15 minutes and return to fire if required. Serve hot to dunk in soup, or with butter.

SERVES 8-10

fireside feast

(D I N N E R)

'Let us permit nature to have her way: she understands
her business better than we do.'

ESSAYS III.XIII MICHEL EYQUEM DE MONTAIGNE (1533-1592)

Farmer's Paella

1kg (2 lb) chicken legs, chopped in half

1 tablespoon paprika

3 tablespoons garlic oil and 8-10 cloves (see note)

1kg (2 lb) pork spare ribs, skin removed
and each rib chopped into three pieces

1 x 1.5kg (3 lb) (New Zealand white) rabbit,
chopped into serving pieces

500g (1 lb) chicken chorizo (or plain chorizo,
or cacciatore)

6 cups (1.5L/48fl oz) chicken stock

1 teaspoon saffron threads

2 Spanish (red) onions, chopped

1 bulb fennel, sliced

1 cup (200g/6½oz) Calasparra rice (Spanish
short-grain white rice, or use Arborio)

2 x 400g (12½oz) cans peeled tomatoes

1 cup chopped Italian (flat-leaf) parsley

Coat chicken with paprika. Heat 2 tablespoons
garlic oil (reserve cloves) in paella pan (or very
large, heavy frying pan). Add chicken and cook
over high heat. Remove from pan to a bowl.
Add pork ribs, rabbit pieces and chorizo in
batches, so as not to crowd pan. Cook meat
and remove from pan to bowl with chicken.

In a billy, heat stock with saffron until
simmering. Keep hot.

Add onion and fennel to paella pan, cook stirring
over a high heat until soft. Add remaining oil and
garlic cloves. Add rice and stir to coat with oil.
Cook 2 minutes, then add tomatoes and their
juice, the parsley and then stir in the hot stock.
Bring to a simmer, then return meat to the pan.
Cook 15-20 minutes over a low heat, stirring
occasionally, until rice is tender.

SERVES 8-10

note: To make garlic oil, roast several heads
of garlic in a 160°C (325°F/Gas Mark 3)
oven for 30–40 minutes. Cut base from
each head, then squeeze individual cloves
into sterilised jars. Cover with olive oil, seal
and store in a cool, dark place.

The meat for this paella can be prepared
and packed in snap-lock plastic bags, then
frozen for transportation and storage.
The chicken with paprika should be packed
separately. Chicken stock in tetra-paks is very
suitable for transportation and can also be
frozen to provide extra 'ice-packs'.

Paella is traditionally cooked on an open
fire using grapevine prunings as fuel. The
aim is to concentrate the heat over the entire
base of the pan. The traditional large shallow
metal paella pan will give the best results,
although a large frying pan could be used if
necessary. Make a ring of stones on which to
sit the pan, and light the fire within this ring.

Brioche Pudding

1 x 450g (14½oz) sweet yellow brioche loaf
150g (5oz) butter, at room temperature
⅓ cup (50g/1½oz) full-cream milk powder
4 eggs
½ nutmeg, freshly grated (or 1 teaspoon ground)
⅔ cup (130g/4½oz) brown sugar
⅔ cup (170ml/5½fl oz) cold water

Slice and generously butter brioche. Re-form the loaf, and place on a double sheet of aluminium foil, which is large enough to wrap it. Dot the top of the loaf with any remaining butter. Bring edges of foil up to form a 'boat' shape, and place this in a fireproof baking dish.

Combine remaining ingredients and beat until smooth. Pour liquid over loaf, encouraging it to penetrate between slices.

Seal foil at centre top of loaf. Place dish

containing packaged loaf in embers, pushing them up to surround it. Cook while main course is being eaten, or at least for 30 minutes. The pudding is ready when liquid has set to a custard. Open package and spoon contents into bowls, topped with a few glacé cumquats and their syrup (recipe following).
SERVES 6-8

note: The brioche can be buttered and wrapped for transportation at home. The remaining ingredients (eggs unbroken) can be stored in a lidded plastic container for mixing with water, as you require.

Glacé Cumquats

1kg (2 lb) cumquats
1 vanilla bean, split
4 cups (880g/28oz) caster sugar
Cold water

Wash cumquats. Prick each one several times with a thin metal trussing skewer, and remove stem end if attached.

Place fruit in a deep saucepan, cover with cold water (there must be enough room for the contents to boil rapidly without spilling over). Bring to the boil, drain. Return fruit to saucepan, cover with cold water by 2cm (¾in). Add vanilla bean. Heat until simmering, then stir in sugar. Simmer, uncovered, for 60-90 minutes, or until cumquats take on a translucent appearance and syrup is thick. Remove from the heat and let syrup settle. Use a slotted spoon to transfer fruit to warm sterilised jars. Pour syrup over to completely cover. Seal and store in a cool dark place until required. Keeps 6-12 months.
MAKES 1KG

Roasted Chestnuts

Score each chestnut with an 'X' at the top and place in a long-handled heavy frying pan (preferably with a perforated base). Roast over very hot coals, shaking pan constantly to move nuts around and achieve an even roasting. The skin will blacken and split when the nuts are ready. Cool a little before peeling, then throw skins in the fire. The chestnuts are good with a little sea salt.

Mulled Wine

3 medium oranges

1 medium thin-skinned lemon

2 x 750ml (24fl oz) bottles dry red wine

1 cup (220g/6½oz) raw sugar

1 tablespoon black peppercorns

10 cloves

4 star anise

1 cinnamon stick

¼ teaspoon freshly grated nutmeg

Using a zester, remove peel from two of the oranges and the lemon. Place this in a camp kettle (with strainer spout) or a clean, non-greased cooking pot.

Squeeze juices from the two oranges and lemon and add to kettle, with remaining ingredients (except reserved orange). Hang kettle on a tripod hook over fire. Bring wine to a simmer, gently shaking kettle or pot until sugar is dissolved. Simmer a few more minutes, then move kettle or pot to a cooler part of the fire to keep warm and let the flavours infuse.

Cut remaining orange into thin wedges, place these in serving cups or heatproof glasses and strain wine over them.

MAKES 1.5L (48fl oz)

one pot wonder

(DINNER)

'And this our life, exempt from public haunt,
Finds tongues in tree, books in the running brooks,
Sermons in stones, and good in everything.'

AS YOU LIKE IT, II.I. WILLIAM SHAKESPEARE (1564-1616)

Lamb Tagine

1.5kg (3 lb) leg of lamb, boned and
　cut into 2.5cm (1in) dice
2 Spanish (red) onions, peeled
　and quartered
2 cloves garlic, peeled
1 cup chopped Italian (flat-leaf) parsley
1 cup roughly chopped coriander
1 x 2.5cm (1in) knob green ginger,
　peeled and quartered
1 teaspoon powdered cumin
¼ teaspoon saffron colouring
1 teaspoon salt
¾ cup (190ml/6fl oz) olive oil
200g (6½oz) packet dried green peas
2 x 300g (9½oz) cans chickpeas
100g (3½oz) preserved or pickled lemons
Ground black pepper to taste

Place lamb in a large snap-lock plastic bag or plastic container.

Combine remaining ingredients, except chickpeas and green peas and lemon, in a blender or food processor and process to a fairly smooth consistency. Pour over the lamb, seal bag and 'massage' to coat meat in paste. The mixture can be frozen at this stage, and transported as an 'ice-pack' amongst other food.

To cook, heat a camp-oven or other heavy pot over the fire. Add thawed meat mixture, dried peas and enough water to barely cover the mixture. Stir, then cover and cook at a simmer for 45 minutes.

Stir in chickpeas and their liquid and cook until they are heated through, with pot uncovered for this part of the cooking. Discard flesh from preserved lemon, slice peel and add to pot. Season with salt and freshly ground black pepper to taste. Serve Tagine with buttery cous cous (recipe following).
SERVES 8-10

Buttery Cous Cous

4 cups (1L/1³⁄₄ pints) chicken stock
90g (3oz) butter
Finely grated rind 1 lemon
2 cardamom pods
500g (1 lb) packet instant cous cous

Heat stock with butter, rind and cardamom in a billy or pot, hanging over flames from a tripod hook. When simmering, pour in cous cous and cover immediately. Remove to a cool part of the fire and stand until required. The cous cous will swell and absorb all the liquid. There is no need to stir it. Serve with the Lamb Tagine.
SERVES 8-10

Pears Baked with Ginger, Maple and Walnut Syrup

6-8 firm Honey, Paradise or Comice pears
125g (4oz) butter, at room temperature
6-8 cubes glacé ginger
2 tablespoons maple syrup
¹⁄₄ cup (40g/1¹⁄₂oz) walnut pieces

Use an apple corer to core pears.

Combine remaining ingredients in a blender or food processor and work to a paste. Fill cavity of each pear with mixture, and then wrap each pear in one layer of baking paper and three thicknesses of aluminium foil, to make a 'pouch' shape. Pears can be refrigerated and packed for transportation at this stage. If kept cool, the filling will remain firm.

To cook, place pears in hot embers at the edge of the fire, bury them and bake for 40-60 minutes. Unwrap carefully to serve; the pear juices will have combined with the filling to make a sauce. Eat while warm.
SERVES 6-8

holiday house cooking

backs to the sun (late breakfast)

with a jigsaw puzzle (morning tea)

with red wine (lunch)

by lamplight (dinner)

~

winter walks

misty morning warmers (brunch)

before the rain (morning tea)

in the orange grove (lunch)

cloud watching (afternoon tea)

winter

backs to the sun

(L A T E   B R E A K F A S T)

'Why, sometimes I've believed as many as six impossible things before breakfast.'

THROUGH THE LOOKING-GLASS LEWIS CARROLL (1832-1898)

Rhubarb and Sago Cups

750g (1 lb/24oz) rhubarb, trimmed,
    washed and cut into 2cm (³⁄₄in) pieces
½ cup (110g/3½oz) brown sugar
½ cup (125ml/4fl oz) mandarin, tangelo
    or orange juice
⅓ cup (70g/2½oz) sago (tapioca seed)
3 cups (750ml/24fl oz) milk
1 teaspoon pure vanilla essence
Fresh berries, to serve

Combine rhubarb, sugar and juice in a deep saucepan. Cover, then cook over a medium heat, stirring occasionally, for 15-20 minutes, or until broken down. You will have about 2 cups (500ml/16fl oz) cooked.

Combine sago, milk and vanilla essence in a deep saucepan. Stir over medium heat until simmering, then cook slowly, stirring frequently, for 20 minutes, until sago is clear and mixture has thickened.

Stir cooked rhubarb and citrus juice into sago. Spoon into individual moulds or glasses (or one large dish) cool and refrigerate until required. (This will keep refrigerated for one week). Transport in moulds. Serve with fresh berries.
MAKES ABOUT 6 CUPS (1.5L/48FL OZ)

note: Persimmon pulp or fresh berries can be used instead of rhubarb. Freeze fruits in small containers, for use out of season.

Individual Onion Bread Puddings

250g (8oz) butter
8 brown onions, coarsely chopped,
    to give about 8 cups
1 teaspoon freshly grated nutmeg
2½ cups (600ml/1 pint/20fl oz) buttermilk
4 eggs, lightly beaten
1 teaspoon salt
¼ teaspoon ground cloves
½ teaspoon freshly ground black pepper
1 x 450g (14½oz) sweet yellow brioche,
    thinly sliced (or white bread)

Melt half the butter in a heavy-based frying pan.
Add onion and nutmeg, stir to coat with butter,
then cover and cook over a low heat, shaking pan
occasionally, for 20 minutes. The onions will be
golden and soft. (You can prepare recipe to this
stage and refrigerate onion until required.)
    Preheat oven to 160°C (325°F/Gas Mark 3).
    Melt reserved butter and whisk with remaining
ingredients, except brioche and onion mixture.
    Butter 8 x 1 cup (250ml/8fl oz) ramekin dishes.
Cut brioche into circles to fit dishes. Place a slice
in base of each ramekin, spoon in some onion
mixture, top with bread and continue until
ramekin is three-quarters full. Pour egg mixture
into ramekins, using a metal spatula to encourage
it to penetrate down to base of dishes.
    Place ramekins in a deep baking dish; pour in
hot water to come halfway up sides of dishes.
Bake uncovered for 45 minutes, or until custard is
set and tops feel firm to touch. Serve immediately.
SERVES 8

note: The puddings can be cooked in
advance, refrigerated and reheated before
serving. They won't be as puffed as when
freshly baked, but are just as delicious.

Roasted Bacon and Tomatoes

750g (1½ lb/24oz) bacon, in one piece
6 sprigs rosemary
8 firm, ripe tomatoes

Preheat oven to 160°C (325°F/Gas Mark 3).
Place bacon on rosemary in a baking dish.
Arrange tomatoes around bacon and bake,
uncovered, for 45 minutes. Serve bacon cut
into thick slices, with tomatoes.

Grapefruit Juice

8 large grapefruit
½ cup (125ml/4fl oz) warmed honey
2 tablespoons orange flower water, if desired

Squeeze the juice from grapefruit through
a sieve into a jug. Stir in warmed honey, and
orange flower water, if desired.
SERVES 8

with a jigsaw puzzle

(MORNING TEA)

'Complacencies of the peignoir, and late
Coffee and oranges in a sunny chair'

SUNDAY MORNING WALLACE STEVENS (1879-1955)

Individual Lemon and Vanilla Cheesecakes

Pastry

½ cup (75g/2½oz) plain flour

¼ cup (60g/2oz) caster sugar

1 egg yolk

1 tablespoon lemon juice

60g (2oz) unsalted butter, diced

Filling

500g (1 lb) cream cheese, at room temperature

1 cup (220g/7oz) caster sugar

Seeds from 1 vanilla pod

¼ cup (40g/1½oz) plain flour

Finely grated rind 1 medium lemon

1 teaspoon lemon juice

3 eggs

¼ cup (60ml/2fl oz) thickened cream

To make pastry, combine flour and sugar in a bowl. Make a well in the centre and add yolk, lemon juice and butter. Using your fingertips, mix ingredients until dough clings together in a ball. Wrap in plastic and refrigerate for 20 minutes.

For filling, beat cream cheese with sugar and vanilla seeds in an electric mixer, or with a wooden spoon, until pale and fluffy. Beat in flour, lemon rind and juice. Add eggs one at a time, beating well after each addition. Stir in cream.

Preheat oven to 200°C (400°F/Gas Mark 5).

Roll pastry between two sheets of baking paper. Rub 6 x 1 cup (250ml/8fl oz) metal dariole moulds with buttered paper. Use one mould to cut pastry circles to line bases. Re-roll scraps if necessary.

Pour filling into moulds. Place on a thin baking tray (pizza trays, especially perforated ones, are ideal) and place in centre of preheated oven. Reduce temperature to 150°C (300°F/Gas Mark 2) and bake for 35-40 minutes. Cool in oven with door ajar (this helps any cracks in tops of cheesecakes to settle closed). Refrigerate in moulds, when cool.

Transport cheesecakes in moulds. They will keep refrigerated, for at least one week or frozen for several months.

MAKES 6

Hot Chocolate Brioche

2 cups (300g/9½oz) plain flour

2 tablespoons caster sugar

1 x 7g (¼oz) sachet dried yeast

½ teaspoon salt

Seeds from 1 vanilla bean

4 egg yolks

⅔ cup (160ml/5½fl oz) lukewarm water

100g (3½oz) butter, at room temperature,
    plus extra for brushing tins

50g (1½oz) dark cooking chocolate, chopped

Combine dry ingredients in a large bowl. Make a well in the centre and pour in 3 yolks whisked with barely lukewarm water. Mix with a wooden spoon to combine as much as possible, then work with your hands to form a ball.

Turn onto a lightly floured surface and knead for 3 minutes, until smooth. Knead in the butter, a small knob at a time, until completely incorporated and the dough is glossy and smooth. You will need to constantly dust flour over work surface. This process takes 25 minutes.

Wash a large ceramic or glass bowl in hot water. Dry, then rub the inside surface with buttered paper. Place dough in the bowl, cover with a clean tea towel and stand in a warm, draft-free position for 1½ hours, or until dough is doubled in bulk.

Brush 12 x ½ cup (125ml/4fl oz) muffin tins with butter. Divide dough into 12 equal portions. Cut a teaspoon-sized piece from each portion. Roll both large and small pieces into balls. Place larger pieces in muffin tins. Press your thumb into centre to create a deep indent. Fill this with chocolate. Position small balls of dough on top of chocolate. Use a skewer to pierce through centre of both balls, pushing right through to base. This process helps hold both pieces together.

Whisk remaining yolk with a teaspoon of cold water and brush over surface of brioche. Stand in a warm draft-free position again, until risen, about 20 minutes.

Preheat oven to 180°C (350°F/Gas Mark 4).

Bake brioche for 15–20 minutes, until golden. Serve warm. (Brioche can be frozen and reheated.)

MAKES 12

Apple Slice with Amaretto

Base

125g (4oz) unsalted butter,
    at room temperature

½ cup (100g/3½oz) brown sugar

125g (4oz) blanched almonds, coarsely ground

½ cup (75g/2½oz) self-raising flour

Topping

½ cup (125ml/4fl oz) Amaretto liqueur

60g (2oz) butter, melted

½ cup (100g/3½oz) brown sugar

¼ cup (40g/1½oz) plain flour

4 Golden Delicious apples,
    cored and very thinly sliced

Preheat oven to 180°C (350°F/Gas Mark 4).

To make base, beat butter and brown sugar until smooth. Stir in almonds and then flour.

Press mixture into the base of a 21 x 29cm (8 x 11in) flan tin with removable base. Refrigerate while preparing topping.

Whisk together all topping ingredients except apples. Add apple to mixture and stir gently with a rubber spatula, to coat. Arrange apple slices in three long rows over base (use broken apple pieces underneath whole slices). Drizzle with any remaining Amaretto mixture.

Place in centre of oven, with an aluminium foil-lined tray on shelf below (some liquid may escape through base of flan tin). Bake 40 minutes. Cool and transport in tin. Will keep when refrigerated, covered for several days.

SERVES 8

with red wine

'And in winter, when you draw the wine,
let there be in your heart a song for each cup;
And let there be in the song a remembrance for the autumn
days, and for the vineyard, and for the winepress.'

THE PROPHET KAHLIL GIBRAN (1883-1931)

Rabbit Terrine

1 x 1.5kg (3 lb) (New Zealand white) rabbit

200g (6½oz) veal steak, cubed

30g (1oz) butter

2 medium onions, finely chopped

8 sage leaves, thinly sliced

1 egg

2 tablespoons brandy

Salt and ground black pepper to taste

125g (4oz) pistachio kernels

1 tablespoon green peppercorns

3 fresh bay leaves

200g (6½oz) pork fat

Remove meat from rabbit carcass. Chop it roughly and combine with veal. Pass through a mincer fitted with the coarsest grinder, or process in small batches in a food processor or blender.

Melt butter in a frying pan over low heat. Add onion and cook until soft, stirring frequently, for 5 minutes. Remove from heat and stir in sage.

Whisk together egg, brandy and season with salt and black pepper to taste. Stir into meat with onion mixture, pistachios and peppercorns.

Preheat oven to 160°C (325°F/Gas Mark 3).

Arrange bay leaves decoratively in base of a 5-cup (1.25L/2-pint) ceramic or enamel terrine (or a heavy loaf tin). Remove 'skin' membrane from pork fat. Place pieces of fat on a sheet of plastic wrap on work surface, in a patchwork roughly the shape of the base of the terrine. Cover with plastic wrap and using a rolling pin, press and roll fat to make one piece. Trim edges to size, and lay fat in base of terrine over bay leaves. Use plastic wrap to assist lifting the fat. Repeat with remaining fat, to make a layer to cover the top of meat.

Spoon meat mixture into terrine, packing it down firmly. Cover with a second layer of fat, and then cover closely with aluminium foil. (Cover terrine with lid, if it has one.)

Place terrine in a deep baking dish and pour in enough hot water to come one-third up the side of terrine. Place in oven and bake 1¼ hours.

Remove from oven and cool for 30 minutes. Place weights (see note) on top of terrine and refrigerate for 24 hours. Serve sliced, with bread and salad.

SERVES 8-10

note: Weights can be cans of food placed on top of a piece of cardboard, cut to size. The terrine can be wrapped in plastic and then foil after the initial 24 hours refrigeration, and frozen for 4–6 months.

Spinach and Labna Salad

Labna
1kg (2 lb) good quality plain yoghurt
Olive oil
4-6 sprigs fresh thyme
1 cinnamon stick

Salad
250g (8oz) baby spinach leaves
1 eschalot (shallot), finely diced
Finely grated rind and juice of 1 lemon
Salt and ground black pepper to taste

Prepare labna in advance and use as a pantry stand-by.

Place yoghurt in a jelly bag and suspend over a bowl overnight (at room temperature in the winter; refrigerate if making this in summer). The liquid will drain from the yoghurt, leaving a very solid mixture. Discard liquid. Roll solids into walnut-sized balls. Place these in a sterilised jar, covering with olive oil as you go, and layering with thyme. Add cinnamon stick and then oil to cover. Seal and store in a cool dark place until required.

Combine labna with spinach leaves, eschalot and lemon rind. Whisk some of the oil with lemon juice as a dressing. Season with salt and freshly ground black pepper to taste.

SERVES 8

note: Labna will keep for several months, as long as it is completely immersed in oil, and a clean spoon is used for removal of balls from jar.

In place of a jelly bag, line a colander with muslin and position it over a deep bowl.

Buttermilk Cake

125g (4oz) unsalted butter,
   at room temperature
1¼ cups (275g/9oz) caster sugar
Seeds from 1 vanilla bean
3 free-range eggs
½ cup (125ml/4fl oz) cultured buttermilk
1½ cups (225g/7½oz) self-raising flour
1 tablespoon vanilla sugar

Preheat oven to 160°C (325°F/Gas Mark 3). Line base of a deep 17cm (6½in) springform tin with baking paper. Rub sides of tin with buttered paper.

Beat butter, sugar and vanilla seeds together until pale and fluffy. Add eggs individually, beating well after each addition. Stir in buttermilk and then flour, until just incorporated.

Spoon mixture into prepared tin, sprinkle top with vanilla sugar.

Bake in centre of oven for 55 minutes. Cool in tin for 10 minutes, then remove. Cool on wire rack.

Cake keeps well, refrigerated in an airtight container. Serve sliced with buttermilk ice-cream or cream.

SERVES 8

note: Cultured buttermilk is made by the addition of bacteria to non-fat or low-fat milk, thickening it and giving it a tangy flavour.

Buttermilk Ice-cream

4 eggs
½ cup (110g/3½oz) vanilla sugar
2½ cups (600ml/1 pint/20fl oz)
   cultured buttermilk

Whisk eggs and sugar until pale, thick and fluffy. Add buttermilk and whisk for 3 minutes. Pour into an ice-cream maker and churn according to manufacturer's instructions. Spoon into a container, cover and freeze. Alternatively, pour into a shallow freezer container and freeze until sludgy. Stir with a fork to break up ice crystals then freeze again until sludgy. Repeat process three times before finally freezing.

This ice-cream has a slightly 'sorbet' texture as the fat content is lower than full-cream ice-cream. Wrap container in several sheets of newspaper and place in cool-box with ice, for transportation.

MAKES ABOUT 1L (1¾ pints)

by lamplight

(D I N N E R)

'Now the cleverest thing that I ever did,' he went on after a
pause, 'was inventing a new pudding during the meat-course.'

THROUGH THE LOOKING-GLASS LEWIS CARROLL (1832-1898)

Oxtail in Red Wine and Mushrooms

1.5kg (3 lb) oxtail, cut into 2cm (¾in) pieces

1 cup (150g/5oz) plain flour

    (or ½ cup gluten-free flour or potato flour

    (starch) and ½ cup maize cornflour)

½ cup (125ml/4fl oz) olive oil

1 medium onion, chopped

1 leek, white and pale green parts chopped

2 cloves garlic, chopped

500g (1 lb) mushrooms (pine, cèpe,

    Swiss brown, field or a mixture), diced

1½ cups (375ml/12fl oz) beef stock

1 x 50g (1½oz) sachet tomato paste

2 tablespoons veal glacé (see note)

3 cups (750ml/24fl oz) red wine

Fresh sprigs thyme, for garnish

Place oxtail, flour and 1 teaspoon of both salt and
freshly ground black pepper in a large plastic bag
(check there are no holes in base). Hold bag
closed and shake to coat meat with flour.

Heat oil in a large, deep, lidded ovenproof pot.
Brown meat in batches, over medium heat.
Remove from pot and set aside. (Reserve bag with
remaining flour.)

Preheat oven to 150°C (300°F/Gas Mark 2).

Add onion, leek and garlic to pot and stir until
softened, about 2 minutes. Increase heat, stir in
mushrooms and cook a further 2 minutes. Stir
in remaining flour, and then add stock, tomato
paste, veal glacé and wine. Bring to a simmer for
5 minutes, stirring occasionally and scraping
browned bits from base of pan. Add oxtail, turning
each piece to cover with liquid. Cover pot and
place in oven. Cook 3 hours, until mixture is thick
and meat is tender and sticky.

SERVES 6-8

note: Make this dish ahead and refrigerate
or freeze. It can be reheated in the oven.

Veal glacé is a very reduced jellied veal stock,
which solidifies when cold. Used in small
amounts, it is an excellent flavour booster.
It can be purchased in small jars from good
delicatessens and butchers.

Saffron Spaetzle with Garlic Butter

1 tablespoon saffron threads (or saffron colour
    powder if threads unavailable)
3 cups (450g/14oz) plain flour
1 teaspoon salt
6 eggs
60g (2oz) butter
1 clove garlic, crushed and finely chopped

Soak saffron in 1 cup (250ml/8fl oz) hot water
until water is lukewarm.

Combine flour and salt in a large bowl. Make a
well in the centre, break in eggs and whisk with a
fork to break up, then add saffron and water. Stir
into flour with a wooden spoon, until smooth.

Bring a large pot of water to the boil. Place
butter and garlic in serving dish in a 150°C
(300°F/Gas Mark 2) oven. Pour ¼ of the flour
mixture into a large-holed colander, as you hold it
over the pot of simmering water. Using a rubber
spatula, push mixture through colander so it falls
into the water. Spaetzle will quickly float to
surface. Scoop out spaetzle with a slotted spoon
and place in serving dish, stirring to coat with
garlic butter. Keep warm while cooking remaining
mixture. Covered spaetzle can be kept warm in
low oven until required. You may wish to sprinkle
it with a little sea salt before serving.
SERVES 6-8

note: Fresh herbs can be added to butter in
serving dish.

Winter Watercress and Fennel Salad

2-3 cups watercress sprigs, washed and drained
1 medium fennel bulb
Finely julienned rind and juice 1 lemon
¼ cup (60ml/2fl oz) walnut oil

Place watercress on serving plate. Trim fennel and
slice very thinly (use a mandolin for best results).
Toss with lemon rind and juice. Scatter over
watercress, cover with plastic and refrigerate until
required. (Watercress wilts quickly at room
temperature.) Sprinkle with walnut oil to serve.
SERVE 6-8

note: Diced preserved lemon rind, and/or
roasted walnut pieces, can be added to the
salad. A mandolin or v-cutter is the best
way of achieving very fine, even slicing.

Paradise Pear Pudding with Calvados

8 small ripe, firm Paradise pears
4 eggs
½ cup (100g/3½oz) brown sugar
1 teaspoon freshly grated nutmeg
¼ cup (60ml/2fl oz) pure maple syrup
¼ cup (60ml/2fl oz) Calvados or brandy
90g (3oz) butter, melted and cooled
½ cup (75g/2½oz) plain flour
    (gluten-free is also suitable)
Clotted cream to serve

Preheat oven to 150°C (300°F/Gas Mark 2).
   Wash pears and place upright in a deep baking
dish just large enough to give a snug fit. Bake
for one hour, uncovered. (The pears will shrink
slightly and fit better if tight in the dish
before cooking.)
   Whisk eggs, brown sugar and nutmeg until thick
and pale. Whisk in maple syrup, Calvados and then
melted butter. Whisk in flour.
   Remove pears from oven. Carefully pour
prepared mixture into hot dish around pears. (Any
excess can be baked separately in a ramekin.)
Return to oven and bake 30 minutes, until filling
is puffed and centre firm to touch.
   Serve hot, with clotted cream.
SERVES 8

note: This can be cooked in the same oven
as the oxtail recipe (see p139). The pudding
looks best when served immediately, when it
is puffed, but is quite acceptable if kept warm
in the turned-off oven. The flavour
is certainly as good.

misty morning warmers

'One misty, moisty morning,
When cloudy was the weather.
There I saw an old man,
Dressed all in green leather.'

ANON (OLD NURSERY RHYME)

Baked Tomato Slice

60g (2oz) butter, melted

8 slices white bread, crusts removed

300g (10oz) firm ripe small tomatoes

6 eggs

1 teaspoon salt

1 teaspoon coarsely ground black pepper

1 teaspoon curry powder

½ cup (125ml/4fl oz) cultured buttermilk

1 cup (115g/3½oz) grated cheddar cheese

Preheat oven to 200°C (400°F/Gas Mark 5).

Generously brush base and sides of a 4 x 18 x 28cm (1½ x 7 x 11in) baking tin with melted butter.

Cut 4 slices of bread to fit base of tin. Layer sliced tomatoes on top, then cover with remaining bread. Press down over entire surface.

Whisk together eggs, salt, pepper, curry powder and buttermilk. Stir in cheese.

Pour over bread. Press down with a rubber spatula. Bake 15 minutes, reduce heat to 180°C (350°F/Gas Mark 4) and bake a further 10 minutes, until puffed and browned. Cool in tin.

Cut into slices and pack in a carry container.

SERVES 6-8

Scotch Eggs

6 eggs

9 thick sausages (about 1kg/2lb),
    choose a flavour you prefer

1 cup (115g/3½oz) packaged dry breadcrumbs

2 cups (500ml/16fl oz) vegetable oil

Boil eggs for 4 minutes, stirring gently for the first minute, to centre yolk. Cool and peel. Dry eggs with a paper towel.

Remove skins from sausages. Using 1½ sausages per egg, shape meat into a disc, wrap egg and smooth edges to give an even-shaped oval. Roll in breadcrumbs to coat well.

Pour oil in a deep frying pan over a medium heat, shallow-fry Scotch eggs, turning frequently, for 10 minutes in total. Drain on paper towels.

Wrap each egg in a napkin or waxed paper for transportation. The eggs keep well, refrigerated, for up to three days.

MAKES 6

note: For a light lunch, serve sliced eggs with finely shredded white cabbage and a dressing of good quality mayonnaise mixed with a tangy chutney or smoked tomato sauce (see recipe p38).

High-top Lemon and Currant Buns

2½ cups (375g/12oz) self-raising flour
½ cup (110g/3½oz) caster sugar
100g (3½oz) butter
1 cup (150g/5oz) currants
Finely grated rind 2 lemons
⅓ cup (90ml/3fl oz) lemon juice
1 egg
1 cup (250ml/8fl oz) buttermilk

Preheat oven to 190°C (375°F/Gas Mark 4).

Cut 6 x postage stamp-size pieces of baking paper and place in each base of 6 x ¾ cup (190ml/6fl oz) baba tins (7cm high x 7cm top width x 5.5cm base width). Cut 8cm wide strips of paper, and roll into tubes then place in tins to line them.

Combine flour, caster sugar and butter in a bowl. Rub in butter until mixture resembles coarse breadcrumbs. Stir in currants and rind. Make a well in the centre, add juice, break in egg and pour in buttermilk. Whisk liquid with a fork, then stir in flour until incorporated.

Spoon mixture into tins to fill each one. Place tins on a thin baking tray (a pizza tray, especially one with a perforated base, is ideal) and cook for 25 minutes until well risen and golden. Cool in tins, then remove and pack, with wrapping intact, in a container for transportation.
MAKES 6

note: If you don't have the baba tins, make mixture as muffins in a 12-hole large muffin tray lined with paper cups. Bake 15–20 minutes.

Chocolate chips can be substituted for the currants for a totally different bun.

You can tie the wrapping on the cooked buns with string.

Hot Chocolate Touched by Rum

Milk to desired quantity
Chocolate powder to taste
Dark rum to taste

Heat milk to scalding point, whisk in chocolate powder and rum to taste. Pour into a warmed thermos.

before the rain

(M O R N I N G   T E A)

'I love the rain, so dear, so fresh,
The long lines running like the warp of a mesh,
Straight out of heaven, down to the earth,
That the flower may bud, and the root have birth.'

RAIN DAME MARY GILMORE (1835-1962)

Salmon and Chive Omelette
in Lemon Ricotta Rolls

6 eggs
30g (1oz) butter
1 bunch chives, chopped
Sea salt and freshly ground black pepper
250g (8oz) fresh ricotta
Finely grated rind and juice of 2 lemons
6 soft white rolls (baps)
12-18 slices smoked salmon

To make omelettes, whisk eggs in a small jug.
Heat a non-stick frying pan over a medium heat.
Melt a small piece of the butter and spread over
surface of the pan. Pour in a little egg mixture,
tilting pan so that egg thinly coats entire surface.
Sprinkle with chives, salt and pepper. Cook until
top is set, turn out by inverting pan onto a board
or work surface. Repeat with remaining egg
mixture, to give six omelettes. Roll each one, and
slice into 2cm (¾in) wide ribbons.

Beat ricotta with lemon rind and juice.

To assemble rolls, cut each in half, spread both
halves with ricotta. On the base half, layer
omelette, then salmon. Place top on roll, and
either wrap individually or place in a napkin-lined
container for transportation.

MAKES 6 ROLLS

Chocolate and Dried Fruit Slice

Base
125g (4oz) butter, at room temperature
½ cup (100g/3½oz) brown sugar
2 eggs
1 cup (150g/5oz) plain flour
½ cup (75g/2½oz) self-raising flour
½ cup (75g/2½oz) drinking chocolate
1 cup (75g/2½oz) desiccated coconut

Topping
3 eggs
125g (4oz) butter, melted
⅓ cup (65g/2½oz) brown sugar
1 tablespoon self-raising flour
1 teaspoon vanilla essence
600g (1¼lb) dried fruit salad,
    cut into 1cm (½in) dice
250g (8oz) chocolate bits

Preheat oven to 190°C (375°F/Gas Mark 4).

Rub two 27 x 18 x 4cm (11 x 7 x 1½in) baking tins with buttered paper.

For base, beat butter and brown sugar until pale and fluffy. Add eggs, one at a time, beating well after each addition. Sift in combined flours and drinking chocolate, then stir in coconut.

Press mixture in base of tins. Bake 10 minutes.

Meanwhile, prepare topping. Whisk eggs, butter, sugar, flour and vanilla until thick and pale. Stir in dried fruit and chocolate bits. Pour over hot cooked base and return to oven for 20 minutes, or until filling is set in centre. Remove from oven and cool in tins. Slice and pack into a container for travelling.

MAKES 20 PIECES

Blood Orange Poppyseed Loaf

½ cup (80g/2½oz) poppy seeds
¼ cup (60ml/2fl oz) milk
150g (5oz) butter, at room temperature
½ cup (110g/3½oz) caster sugar
Grated rind and juice 2 blood oranges
    (or lemons or orange), to give ⅔ cup
    (180ml/6fl oz) juice
1½ cups (225g/7oz) self-raising flour
1 cup (250ml/8fl oz) plain natural yoghurt

Preheat oven to 160°C (325°F/Gas Mark 3).

Rub inside a 6 cup (1.5L/48fl oz) loaf tin with buttered paper. Line the tin with one length of baking paper, overlapping each long side.

Combine poppy seeds and milk in a small bowl and microwave for 1 minute, or heat gently in a small saucepan. Cool.

Beat butter and sugar until pale and fluffy. Stir poppy seeds into butter, then beat in orange rind and juice. Stir in flour and yoghurt in three lots, ending with flour, to give a smooth batter.

Pour into tin. Bake 70-75 minutes, until loaf tests done. Cool in tin. Wrap in waxed paper and foil for transportation.

SERVES 8-10

note: Glaze cake if you wish with a thin paste of icing sugar and blood orange juice.

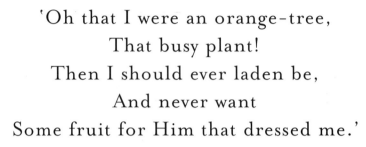

in the orange grove

(L U N C H)

'Oh that I were an orange-tree,
That busy plant!
Then I should ever laden be,
And never want
Some fruit for Him that dressed me.'

EMPLOYMENT GEORGE HERBERT (1593-1633)

Little Olive Tarts

Pastry

1⅓ cup (200g/7oz) plain flour
1 teaspoon cumin
½ teaspoon salt
150g (5oz) unsalted butter
1 tablespoon plain natural yoghurt

Filling

1 tablespoon olive oil
1 bulb fennel, finely diced
500g (1lb) black olives, stoned and chopped

To make pastry, combine flour, cumin and salt in a bowl. Rub in butter until mixture resembles coarse breadcrumbs. Stir in yoghurt, and then work with your fingers until dough clings together. Knead briefly until smooth. Shape into a disc, wrap in plastic and refrigerate 20 minutes.

For filling, heat oil in a pan, add fennel and cook over low heat until beginning to soften. Remove from heat and stir in olives. Cool.

Preheat oven to 190°C (375°F/Gas Mark 4).

Divide pastry into eight pieces. Roll each piece into a ball, then flatten into a circle, about 8cm (3in) in diameter. Place on baking tray, pinch up edge to form a decorative border and prick base with a fork.

Spoon filling into each pastry base. Bake 15-20 minutes, or until pastry is crisp and golden. Cool on tray, then transfer to a container for travelling (layer tarts between sheets of waxed paper).

MAKES 8

note: This pastry can be used with various fillings. Try ricotta and spinach, mushrooms and garlic, diced grilled eggplant with chickpea purée.

Lamb Spice Balls

⅓ cup (50g/2½oz) pinenuts
1 small onion, roughly chopped
¼ teaspoon ground allspice
¼ teaspoon ground cinnamon
A pinch each of ground nutmeg,
    cloves and ginger
Salt and ground black pepper
500g (1lb) minced lamb
1 cup (150g/5oz) potato flour (starch)
⅔ cup (180ml/6fl oz) canola or vegetable oil
⅓ cup (90ml/3fl oz) mustard seed oil

Process pinenuts, onion, spices, salt and freshly ground black pepper to taste together in a food processor (or nut grinder). Stir into meat. Refrigerate 1 hour, if possible. Roll into egg-sized ovals. Coat with potato flour (starch).
  Heat combined oils in a deep frying pan over medium heat. Fry balls in batches until crisp and cooked through. Drain on paper towels. Pack into a container lined with wax paper for transportation. Serve at room temperature.
MAKES ABOUT 20

Cauliflower and Tahini Purée

½ medium cauliflower, cut into florets
    and steamed until tender
⅓ cup (90ml/3fl oz) tahini
⅔ cup (180ml/6fl oz) lemon juice
2 cloves garlic, crushed
1 teaspoon salt

Combine all ingredients in blender and purée to a smooth paste. Add more lemon juice if desired. If too thick, dilute with a tablespoon water. Serve at room temperature. Keeps well for several days in refrigerator. Spoon into a lidded container for transportation.
MAKES ABOUT 2 CUPS

Mint Paste

2 cups mint leaves
⅓ cup (50g/2½oz) pinenuts
Finely grated rind and juice of 1 lemon
1 clove garlic
1 teaspoon ground coriander
1 tablespoon brown sugar
¼ cup (60ml/2fl oz) mustard seed oil
¼ cup (60ml/2fl oz) olive oil

Place all ingredients in a blender. Process until smooth. Transfer to a lidded container for transportation and refrigerate until required.
MAKES ABOUT 1 CUP (250ml/8fl oz)

cloud watching

(A F T E R N O O N   T E A)

'I wandered lonely as a cloud
That floats on high o'er vales and hills.'
I WANDERED LONELY AS A CLOUD WILLIAM WORDSWORTH (1770-1850)

Parmesan Bread

3½ cups (500g/1 lb) unbleached bread flour

1 x 7-8g sachet dried yeast

1½ teaspoons salt

1 teaspoon brown sugar

1 cup (125g/4oz) finely grated Parmesan

1 teaspoon chilli powder

1½ cups (375ml/12fl oz) lukewarm water

Combine all ingredients, except water, in the large bowl of an electric mixer. Make a well in the centre and pour in lukewarm water. Stir to combine, then, using the dough hook, knead 10 minutes. The dough should be of earlobe texture. (This of course can be done by hand.)

Rub inside a large ceramic or glass bowl with buttered paper. Place ball of dough in bowl, rotate it to 'butter' surface. Cover with a clean tea towel and stand in a warm, draft-free position until doubled in bulk, about 60-75 minutes.

Rub inside a bread loaf tin (11 x 18 x 11cm/ 4 x 7 x 4in) with buttered paper.

Punch dough down; knead again for three minutes, until smooth. Divide dough into two and knead each piece into a smooth ball. Place both side-by-side in tin. Cover and stand again, about 30 minutes, or until dough has risen over top edge of tin.

Preheat oven to 200°C (400°F/Gas Mark 5). Brush top of loaf very lightly with cold water, place in oven and bake 40-50 minutes, until dark golden and crisp and loaf pulls away from sides of tin.

Turn out onto a wire rack to cool. Wrap in waxed paper and then foil for transportation.
MAKES 1 LOAF

note: This bread is also good toasted. You may wish to omit the chilli powder if intending to eat it for breakfast.

Roasted Red Capsicum Dip

2 red capsicum (bell peppers)
2 cloves garlic
1 cup (250g/8oz) full-cream fresh ricotta
½ teaspoon freshly ground black pepper
½ cup torn fresh oregano leaves
½ cup stoned black olives, chopped

Heat grill. Halve capsicum lengthways and remove stem, seeds and pith. Place capsicum skin-side-up on grill tray, place under grill until skin blackens and blisters. Transfer to a bowl and cover with a plate until capsicums are cool enough to handle. Peel.

Place capsicum in a blender with any collected juices, the garlic, ricotta and pepper. Blend to a paste, then stir in oregano and olives. Refrigerate, covered, for up to 5 days. Spoon into a lidded container for transportation.

MAKES 2 CUPS

Artichoke and Chèvre Spread

1 cup marinated artichoke hearts, drained
Finely grated rind and juice 1 lemon
150g (5oz) chèvre
1 teaspoon Tabasco sauce
½ teaspoon freshly ground black pepper
¼ cup (60g/2oz) sour cream
½ cup finely chopped dill

Combine all ingredients except dill in a blender and process until fairly smooth. If too thick, add a little artichoke marinade. Stir in dill. Refrigerate, covered, for up to 5 days. Spoon into a lidded container for transportation.

MAKES 2 CUPS

winter walks

winter

Glacé Peach and Coconut Slice

Base
½ cup (75g/2½oz) plain flour
60g (2oz) unsalted butter
2 tablespoons caster sugar
Finely grated rind ½ lemon
1 teaspoon lemon juice
1 free-range egg

Topping
1 x 400g (12½oz) can sweetened
    condensed milk
1 cup (75g/2½oz) desiccated coconut
500g (1 lb) glacé peaches,
    cut into 1cm (½in) dice
3 tablespoons self-raising flour

Preheat oven to 180°C (350°F/Gas Mark 4).

To make base, combine flour, butter and sugar in a bowl. Rub in butter until mixture resembles coarse breadcrumbs. Stir in lemon rind. Whisk lemon juice into egg. Make a well in centre of flour, stir in egg and mix until dough clings together.

Turn into a 28 x 17 x 5cm (11 x 6½ x 2in) baking tin. Press mixture down to cover base evenly. Bake 6 minutes.

Meanwhile, prepare filling. Combine all ingredients and mix well. Pour over hot base, return to oven and bake a further 20 minutes. Cool in tin. Serve cut into slices. Pack into a lidded container for transportation. Keeps well, if refrigerated for 1–2 weeks.

MAKES 20 PIECES

Ginger and Pecan Caramel Squares

Base

1 cup (150g/5oz) self-raising flour

1 cup (220g/7oz) dark brown sugar

125g (4oz) butter, melted

100g (3½oz) pecans, roasted and crushed

Topping

1 x 400g (12½oz) can sweetened
    condensed milk

30g (1oz) butter

200g (6½oz) pecans,
    roasted and coarsely chopped

100g (3½oz) glacé ginger, chopped

60g (2oz) dark chocolate, melted

Preheat oven to 180°C (350°F/Gas Mark 4).

Combine base ingredients and mix well. Press into base of a 28 x 17 x 5cm (11 x 6½ x 2in) baking tin. Bake 10 minutes.

Meanwhile, prepare filling. Combine condensed milk and butter in a heavy-based saucepan. Stir over a moderately low heat until bubbling and thickened, about 8 minutes. Try not to let base catch, but it's not critical, as long as it doesn't burn.

Stir in pecans and ginger and pour over hot base. Return to oven and bake a further 20 minutes. Cool in tin, then drizzle with melted chocolate (place it in a small plastic bag, snip corner to make a tiny hole and use this as a piping bag.) When chocolate has set, cut slice into squares. Keeps well, refrigerated for 1-2 weeks. Pack into a lidded container for transportation.

MAKES 20 PIECES

index